Nevada's Historic Buildings

WILBUR S. SHEPPERSON SERIES IN NEVADA HISTORY

Nevada's Historic Buildings

A CULTURAL LEGACY

Ronald M. James AND
Elizabeth Safford Harvey

PHOTOGRAPHS BY Thomas Perkins

UNIVERSITY OF NEVADA PRESS ▲▲ RENO & LAS VEGAS

Wilbur S. Shepperson Series in Nevada History
Series Editor: Michael Green

University of Nevada Press, Reno, Nevada 89557 USA
Copyright © 2009 by University of Nevada Press
Photographs copyright © by Thomas Perkins
All rights reserved
Manufactured in the United States of America
Design by Kathleen Szawiola

LIBRARY OF CONGRESS CATALOGING-IN-PUBLICATION DATA

James, Ronald M. (Ronald Michael), 1955–
Nevada's historic buildings : a cultural legacy / Ronald M. James and
Elizabeth Safford Harvey ; photographs by Thomas Perkins.
    p. cm. — (Wilbur S. Shepperson series in Nevada history)
Includes bibliographical references and index.
ISBN 978-0-87417-797-8 (hardcover : alk. paper)
ISBN 978-0-87417-798-5 (pbk. : alk. paper)
1. Historic buildings—Nevada. 2. Nevada—History, Local.
3. Nevada—History. I. Harvey, Ann, 1951– II. Perkins, Thomas.
III. Title.
F842.J37 2009
979.3—dc22   2009015670

The paper used in this book is a recycled stock made from 30 percent post-
consumer waste materials, certified by FSC, and meets the requirements of
American National Standard for Information Sciences—Permanence of
Paper for Printed Library Materials, ANSI/NISO z39.48-1992 (R2002).
Binding materials were selected for strength and durability.

FIRST PRINTING

18   17   16   15   14   13   12   11 10 09
5 4 3 2 1

FRONTISPIECE: *Lincoln County Courthouse.*

For Susan, David, and Ellen

Stewart Indian School in Carson City is a rare off-reservation institution
for instructing Native American youth.

Contents

Illustrations

FACING PAGE:

A window and lamp serve as elegant accents for the grand style
of the 1923 Caliente Depot

MAP

Acknowledgments

This work pays tribute to the thousands of volunteers working with the Nevada Commission for Cultural Affairs to preserve the state's rich heritage. Each volunteer has made a difference in his or her own way, and all Nevadans owe them a debt of gratitude. We are particularly grateful to those volunteers who helped us document the histories of their own structures highlighted in the following pages. Of particular note are the photographs of Tom Perkins, who documented the restoration work of the commission. His sensitive images pay homage to the architectural creativity of generations of Nevadans.

We would also like to acknowledge the distinguished Nevadans who have served on the Commission for Cultural Affairs over the past two decades. In particular, we wish to honor the extensive contributions of the commission chairs: Marcia Growden (1991–1994), I. R. Ashleman (1994–1999), and Robert Ostrovsky (serving since 1995, chair since 1999). Their extensive efforts, often hidden from the view of the public, cannot be overestimated. While all of the commissioners have made notable contributions to the state, Robert Stoldal (serving from 1999 to the present) has earned our special thanks for his remarkable support of the commission staff and of its projects.

The Department of Cultural Affairs boasts an array of talented and dedicated staff and administrators, all of whom deserve our acknowledgment. We are particularly grateful to Dr. Michael E. Fischer, currently the department director, for his consistent and thoughtful support of every aspect of the department's activities, including the work of the commission. Moreover, our friends and colleagues in the State Historic Preservation Office, who have lovingly labored for nearly two decades on the commission grants, have also earned our unwavering respect. We want to acknowledge them for their service and thank them for their assistance to the program.

FACING PAGE:
The McKinley Park School was one of four schools built in Reno at the beginning of the twentieth century. Known as the Spanish Quartet for their Mission Revival design, they served for decades, but only two survive.

The commission and its extensive preservation successes would not have come into existence were it not for the visionary efforts of the Nevada state legislature. Bills authorizing and reauthorizing the commission and its grant program have passed the legislature unanimously on almost every occasion. A few legislators deserve individual recognition in this regard. The late Senators Nicholas Horn and Lawrence Jacobsen, Senators William Raggio, Bob Coffin, and Raymond Rawson, Speaker Joe Dini, Assemblyman John Marvel, and Assemblywoman Gene Wines Segerblom were instrumental in advancing the initial legislation that created the Commission for Cultural Affairs. We thank these legislators for their dedication to historic preservation in Nevada, for their guidance, and for their wisdom.

Regarding the publication of the book, we thank the staff of the University of Nevada Press, especially Joanne O'Hare, director; Sara Vélez Mallea, managing editor; Kathleen Szawiola, design and production manager; and Sheryl Laguna, business manager. Annette Wenda made helpful copyediting suggestions. A supportive attitude combined with remarkable expertise make these people valued assets. Nevada is lucky to have such a fine university press.

In addition, our gifted photographer, Tom Perkins, thanks his wife, Ellen, and their children, Elizabeth, Barbara, Molly, Julianne, and Amy.

Finally, the authors wish to thank our spouses, Susan James and David Harvey, and our children, Reed, Rachel, and Michael, for ongoing support in what proved to be too long of a process writing this book. Unending patience is always the greatest gift.

Nevada's Historic Buildings

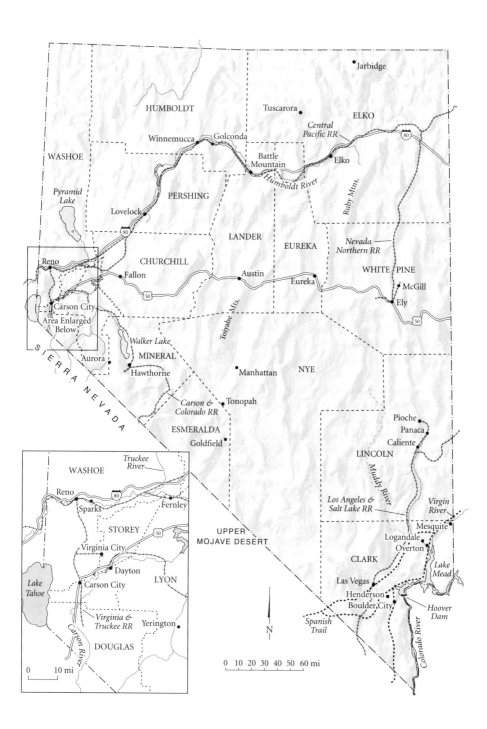

Jarbidge

HUMBOLDT

Tuscarora

ELKO

*Central
Pacific RR*

Winnemucca   Golconda

Battle
Mountain   Elko

WASHOE

Humboldt River

*Pyramid
Lake*

PERSHING

Lovelock

80

Ruby Mtns.

LANDER

EUREKA

*Nevada
Northern RR*

Reno

CHURCHILL

WHITE PINE

Fallon

Austin

Eureka

McGill

50

Carson City

Ely

*Area Enlarged
Below*

50

Walker Lake

Toyabe Mtns.

Aurora   MINERAL
Hawthorne   Manhattan   NYE

Pioche
Panaca
Caliente

*Carson &
Colorado RR*   Tonopah

S
I
E
R
R
A

ESMERALDA
Goldfield

LINCOLN

Muddy River

N
E
V
A
D
A

*Los Angeles &
Salt Lake RR*

*Virgin
River*

Mesquite

Logandale
Overton

*Truckee
River*

WASHOE

80

Reno

Sparks   Fernley

STOREY   50

Virginia City

UPPER
MOJAVE DESERT

CLARK

*Lake
Mead*

Las Vegas

Henderson
Boulder City

*Hoover
Dam*

Dayton

*Lake
Tahoe*   Carson City   LYON

*Virginia &
Truckee RR*   Yerington

Colorado River

Carson River

*Spanish
Trail*

N

DOUGLAS

0   10 mi

0 10 20 30 40 50 60 mi

Introduction

Remnants of Nevada's architectural heritage are scattered like flecks of gold across the state's map. Clinging to the sides of windswept mountains or perched beside desert springs, they bear silent witness to the state's history. When scrutinized, these quiet mementos surviving from earlier times can be made to speak about their eras, providing valuable insights into the development of Nevada's society and culture. For decades, however, many of these aged buildings were abandoned to the corrosive forces of time. As years passed, some succumbed to Nevada's harsh environment. Large portions of the state's cultural heritage were irredeemably lost, and significant evidence about the state's past dissolved into the landscape. Although many have engaged in heroic efforts to preserve some of these vestiges of the past, the demands of time, capital, and architectural expertise have too often spelled disaster for many of Nevada's icons of the past. Despite their best efforts, residents of every community in the state can recall with regret a building torn down.

Two decades ago, a visionary group from Nevada's cultural community including preservationists, museum managers, artists, and performers worked with members of the Nevada state legislature to address the prob-

An antique padlock hangs on a doorsill at the Panaca Heritage Center.

lems confronting the state's stock of historic building. In 1991, a coalition of legislators called for the creation of the Nevada Commission for Cultural Affairs, an agency that would draw on both the public and the private sectors to preserve the best of these resources and to convert them into cultural centers. Two years later, the commission began a bold program of awarding grants to local groups for the rehabilitation of historic buildings to be used as cultural centers. In 1995, the commission began distributing two million dollars annually, and by 2004 dozens of restored historic buildings were welcoming visitors.

Because of this legacy of success, the 2005 legislature reauthorized the program for another decade, increasing its available grants to three million dollars annually. By 2007, after spending more than thirty million dollars, more than eighty impressive architectural resources, each representing significant facets of the state's heritage, had received assistance. Thanks to the dedicated efforts of many people and to funding from the commission, this cooperative effort has produced a remarkable assemblage of preservation successes. Museums, concert halls, theaters, libraries, and small venues of all sorts raise the cultural bar for Nevada and help residents and visitors interpret and understand the region's past.

Key to the commission's work was its collaboration with local people. Each participating community selected the buildings it treasured most and transformed them into cultural centers. Thousands of volunteers handpicked and lovingly toiled over the projects presented here. They imagined that everything from abandoned buildings to dangerous eyesores could be something better. These Nevadans picked what would be included in this book by saving the historic resources most cherished by their communities. Taken together, these refurbished structures represent the best of the survivors. Their stories document the development of the state and highlight key aspects of Nevada's history.

Standing as historical beacons, these structures shed light on the development of the state's culture and illuminate the character of its people. A good part of the American story consists of tales relating to the settlement of a vast continent, the taming of its lands, and the exploitation of its resources to serve the needs of agriculture and industry. Too often, those who arrived in the area now known as Nevada found a parsimonious place that offered little in the way of agricultural bounty and refused to be domesticated. Nevadans have always known that to survive and succeed, they would have to be inventive. It took resourcefulness to build lives where the landscape was a harsh master, and people had to make do with modest buildings cobbled together with whatever they could obtain. The state's architectural history encapsulates, then, core aspects of the Nevada character. It begins with the first settlers' innovative use of the land's scarce resources as they struggled to survive in the region's challenging and often inhospitable environment. And in a postmodern twist, it ends with stories of Nevadans celebrating this very type of inventiveness. In "postmodern Las Vegas," Nevadans have turned their resourcefulness, at first spawned by necessity, into an end in itself. Entrepreneurs market inventiveness to the world, presenting Las Vegas as a global destination where people regard "new" as better not because it is in fact better but because it is simply new.

In its own way, the Commission for Cultural Affairs encapsulates the inventive spirit of Nevadans. The agency was cobbled together with the resources at hand, giving awards to aid scattered buildings that in many cases some argued should have been demolished. But Nevadans have long recognized that a harsh environment demands frugality, and it is better to find a use for a resource than to dispose of it. *Nevada's Historic Buildings: A Cultural Legacy* is a celebration of these resources and of the character of Nevadans who imagined ways to transform an unforgiving landscape into a livable place. The buildings described here provide an opportunity to peer through windows at former times and at people who lived and worked in Nevada as its destiny unfolded. The structures document a century and a half of settlement, development, and change.

While history stands as a witness to change, landscape furnishes its immutable backdrop. Buildings symbolize the drama of history, but much of the Nevada setting has remained constant. The same mountains, valleys, and deserts have witnessed Native Americans, miners, ranchers, railroad workers, divorcées, and gambling executives as they established their places in the state's story.

The first chapter of this book opens with the region's tenuous beginnings. If it had not been for later events, the three buildings it highlights might have served as the foundation for a much different state.

The next chapter charts the dramatic events surrounding some of the greatest mineral strikes the world has ever known. It is the extraordinary story of buildings constructed virtually overnight and seemingly "out of nothing" that demands attention during Nevada's first mining boom. Eleven examples of the state's rich cultural heritage from this first mining era received commission support and are the subject of this chapter. As a group, they illustrate a vibrant period, reminding us that Nevada's mineral wealth and the labor of its early miners defined the state's first economic boom. Sites ranging from Pioche to the Comstock and from Tuscarora to Austin constitute bright spots on the state's cultural terrain. Because structures built during the nineteenth-century period of prosperity often outlived the communities that created them, commission support was essential for preserving this important aspect of the past.

The front facade of Piper's Opera House dates to 1863, during the Nevada territorial period. The theater is one of the more famous of its kind in the nation.

The other side of early Nevada is the subject of the third chapter. Eleven additional structures dating from the 1860s to the turn of the century serve as examples of how the state developed its non-mining infrastructure and began diversifying its economy. Ranchers, railroad men, tradespeople, merchants, and innkeepers also helped shape Nevada, and

A beautiful stone arch at the Logandale School exhibits the sort of craftsmanship often associated with historic structures.

like the miners, they made enduring contributions to its character and cultural heritage. Places as diverse as Reno, Mesquite, Lovelock, and Elko served as urban centers to a large part of Nevada. These communities did not decline with the failure of mines. Due to funding from the commission, the buildings highlighted in this chapter illustrate the diversification of Nevada's economy as an innovative response to the economic malaise accompanying the decline of Nevada's first mines.

Chapter 4 begins with the turn of the century and Nevada's second great mining boom, the last great mineral rush of the continental United States. Tonopah and Goldfield present charming images of this glorious time. The wealth of these mining capitals affected the entire region, and their legacy is inscribed in the architecture of Nevada's Progressive Era. In many ways, the state's early-twentieth-century mining boom mirrored its nineteenth-century predecessor, but by this time Nevada's economy was more complex.[1] Though turn-of-the-century buildings often reflect the opulence of the new mining discoveries, they also testify to an increasing reliance on agriculture and the transportation industry. In addition, they provide clues as to how the Progressive movement shaped the state's cultural life. Roughly two dozen buildings illustrate this period.

Chapter 5 begins with the 1920s and another period of economic change. This was an era of cultural experimentation and economic challenges, when Nevadans once again found innovative solutions to social and economic problems. The state turned to the divorce industry and eventually to gaming, while some residents also began marketing their state's Wild West image as a tourist attraction. Twelve historic buildings document this dynamic period of growth and diversification. People have only recently recognized the historic importance of the buildings constructed during this exciting time. Although these resources could have been lost to demolition, local groups have transformed them into cornerstones of Nevada's cultural map.

Just as the state was turning to gaming to address the economic downturn of the Great Depression, the federal government implemented the

Antique trunks are part of the display inside Boulder City's 1931 Union Pacific Railroad Depot.

New Deal. Publicly funded projects during the 1930s constituted a distinct phase of Nevada's architectural history, providing the subject for chapter 6. Responding to economic challenges, federal agencies worked with Nevadans to create jobs. Construction projects were essential to this collaboration. These projects included the taming of the Colorado River with the Hoover Dam, a reclamation project that was initiated before the 1929 stock market crash. An architectural marvel in its own right, the dam's presence and its economic contribution to southern Nevada spawned the construction of numerous other public and private buildings and structures throughout the region. Federal programs including the New Deal made substantial contributions to Nevada's cultural life during the 1930s, but their social and economic impact was even more significant. Federal projects not only supplied jobs for unemployed Nevadans but also attracted thousands of other workers to the state. Many of the new arrivals chose to remain in Nevada after their projects ended.

Chapter 7 addresses the prosperity that Nevada experienced during the last half of the twentieth century, another era of cultural innovation. Tourism had played an important role in the state's economic life since the late 1920s. As people enjoyed more opportunities to travel, Nevada, and in particular Las Vegas, became a celebrated destination. Having learned through the decades how best to accommodate its guests, the state's tourism industry emerged as a national and even an international leader in the field.

As has been the case during each period of the state's history, Nevada's innovative spirit was reflected in its postwar architecture. During the late 1940s and continuing into the twenty-first century, the state's modern, ultramodern, and postmodern structures inspired the nation's leading architects, winning Nevada a unique place in the history of design. Robert Venturi, Denise Scott Brown, and Steven Izenour's 1972 book, *Learning from Las Vegas*, one of the classic statements of postmodern aesthetic, celebrated Las Vegas's diverse architectural forms and suggested architects could learn from the city's artful constructs. Recognizing the historic importance of Las Vegas's innovative buildings, the Commission for Cultural Affairs assisted six restoration efforts focusing on structures that were constructed during the postwar era. Underscoring both the problems and the promises associated with historic preservation in a rapidly developing region, of these six structures, one burned down and another failed as a cultural center, but the other four have promising futures. These more recent additions to the ever-expanding list of successful commission projects help round out the architectural history of Nevada.

Taken as a whole, the resources described in this book provide a cross section of Nevada's heritage. Emerging from a process of local planning and statewide evaluation, these buildings are among the best in the state. As a whole, these theaters, homes, businesses, courthouses, churches, and schools illustrate a rich history typified by a creative character, but even more, they provide everyone with an opportunity to touch the past. The stories of the people and events that shaped Nevada can be provocative and inspiring. Yet no narrative, however informative, can replace the enthralling experience of walking into a building and viewing the site where a people's history was made.

1 A Territory of Humble Beginnings

Early trappers and explorers crossed what would become Nevada during the 1830s and 1840s. The cliché of the westward movement, as summarized by Frederick Jackson Turner in his renowned frontier thesis, would have farmers follow the pathfinders, from the Atlantic, across the country, to the Pacific Ocean. The Great Basin and the Upper Mojave Desert, however, enjoyed a different history.[1] There, rugged mountains and vast deserts did not attract many interested in agriculture.

The lands lying between the deserts of the Great Salt Lake and the Sierra Nevada were first penetrated by mountain men and fur traders in the 1820s. Military adventurers and a handful of California-bound emigrants explored the region in the 1830s and 1840s, blazing trails as they progressed through the Great Basin's desert wastes. These trails were followed by the next wave of emigrants to traverse the region. This group, composed primarily of gold-seeking "forty-niners," was interested, like those who had preceded them, more in making their fortunes in California than in settling in the arid deserts lying east of the Sierra Nevada.

A few followers of the Church of Jesus Christ of Latter-day Saints, popularly known as Mormons, settled around Las Vegas Springs in the

1850s. At the same time, Mormons and others arrived at the eastern foot of the Sierra. In both areas, the newcomers hoped as much to capitalize on the overland trade as to cultivate the area's too often uncooperative soil. A smattering of other farmers and ranchers tried their luck, but most who braved the harsh environment between the Great Salt Lake and Carson Valley traversed the region as quickly as possible on their way to California. The patterns of the area's early development departed, therefore, from the norm and stamped the future Silver State with an identity uniquely its own.[2]

The region's character was a creation of place and process or, as Turner would put it, of "land and people."[3] Less than a decade elapsed between the founding of the western Great Basin's first Euro-American settlements and the emergence of its first industrial cities. This rapid leap from rugged frontier settlements to modern industrial communities imparted an ephemeral quality to Nevada's mining towns. These seemingly precarious outposts of nineteenth-century industrial society were engulfed by vast stretches of wilderness. This juxtaposition of land and people made the Nevada landscape seem more foreboding and omnipresent than the "tamed" lands that harbored the nation's other nineteenth-century industrial and agricultural communities. In Nevada, nature assumed an eternal and omnipotent tone, whereas its newly established settlements appeared immature and vulnerable.

Perhaps due to this dichotomy, society in the Great Basin assumed a youthful air. Unlike the "mature" communities that developed slowly in other regions of the country, society in Nevada did not take itself too seriously. This aspect of the state's character—its acceptance of the precariousness of the human condition and the timelessness of the land—became its strength and, ultimately, its destiny. Youthful experimentation, play, and innovation are central to the state's character, and out of these qualities Nevada's legendary "freewheeling" morality, cultural ambivalence, and openness to strangers of all types would emerge.

A key to understanding Nevada's character can be found, then, in its early mining camps. Gold and silver strikes spawned mining throughout the territory. By the time Nevada became a state in 1864, boomtowns were scattered across its landscape, a phenomenon that set it apart from much of the rest of the United States. Although these industrial enclaves distinguished early Nevada from other frontier regions, the contemporary view generally asserted that the place had little other use. The great English explorer Richard F. Burton expressed a popular sentiment when he largely condemned the Great Basin in 1860. "All was desert: the bottom could [not] be called basin or valley: it was a fine silt, thirsty dust in the dry season, and putty-like mud in the spring and autumnal rains. The hair of this unlovely skin was sage and greasewood: it was warted with sand-heaps; in places mottled with bald and horrid patches of salt soil, whilst in others minute crystals of salt, glistening like diamond-dust in the sunlight, covered tracts of moist and oozy mud."[4]

In spite of this, even Burton went on to admit there were "small sweet springs." Still, the fertile lands of the Sacramento Valley just across the mountains and the discovery of gold at Sutter's Mill in 1848 inspired most people to see California as more enticing than the desert wastes that immigrant trails traversed across what would become Nevada. Besides the Mormon pioneers, there was a scattering of other traders and farmers who attempted to support themselves by exploiting commercial opportunities offered by the trade routes crisscrossing the Great Basin. Together, these pioneers established the region's first non–Native American settlements.

Ironically, it was the exhaustion of California placer mining that inspired renewed attention to the eastern Sierra slope. Many who had crossed the Great Basin on their way to California during the Gold Rush now hoped to exploit new diggings east of the Sierra crest. The region emerged as a last-chance refuge for failed forty-niners. This circumstance initiated a connection between the two sides of the mountain range that frequently made what would become Nevada subservient to and often dependent on its more prosperous neighbor. In time it even inspired an unflattering characterization of the region as a colony of California.[5]

Although many initially dismissed the Great Basin and the Upper Mojave Desert as uninhabitable, those who settled there became adroit at exploiting the land's often meager resources. Whether their communities flourished or waned, Nevada's early residents left their mark on the landscape. Buildings surviving from this early period offer a chance for insight into the first chapter of the territory's story, beginning more than 150 years ago.

Three of Nevada's older buildings, located at opposite ends of the state, demonstrate that both success and failure are possible when dealing with fragile resources. These structures are tied by reality or tradition to the territorial period, and the way they have been preserved says a great deal about the way later generations would look at their past and incorporate early remnants of the period into their folklore. Regardless of how people perceive them, the Kiel Ranch in North Las Vegas, the Foreman-Roberts House in Carson City, and the courthouse in Genoa represent early attempts to establish agricultural and trading communities as the backbone of their region's development.

Not surprisingly, early settlements were situated near reliable sources of water, the desert's most valuable natural resource.[6] The Kiel Ranch, the original site of the Foreman-Roberts House, and Genoa were close to the great overland trade routes traversing the West, tying each place to an important early chapter in Nevada and national history. These three sites also speak to the extremes of Nevada landscape and history. They underscore the diversity of social roles and cultural traditions that flourished on the Nevada frontier.

KIEL RANCH

The Kiel Ranch in North Las Vegas is located in the Mojave Desert, one of the world's most arid landscapes. The secret of survival in this harsh terrain has always been water, and the Kiel Ranch was ideally situated at one of the Las Vegas Valley's most reliable artesian springs. This was one of several water sources in the area, the chief of which came to be known as the Las Vegas Springs, about three miles southwest of Kiel Ranch.[7]

Archaeological evidence suggests Native Americans used these local springs at least two thousand years before Spanish explorers traversed the region. Early-nineteenth-century Mexican adventurers and traders watered at the Las Vegas Springs on their way from New Mexico to California along the Spanish Trail. Later, mountain men and military explorers from the United States found respite at the various watering holes.[8]

William Bringhurst and his party of Mormon missionaries followed the Spanish Trail into the Las Vegas Valley in June 1855. Unlike many who preceded them, however, they planned to stay. Hoping to expand and establish the extent of "Deseret," the proposed Mormon empire, the settlers built a fort about three miles east of the springs, dug irrigation trenches, and began raising crops. By dominating local water sources, they were in a position to control trade, agricultural products, and, of course, the water itself. The missionaries imagined that the conversion of the local Southern Paiutes would be a by-product of their labors. Although they succeeded in

Many regard the simple adobe structure at Kiel Ranch as one of the oldest buildings in Nevada. Even though it is protected from the elements, the artifact may not survive.

establishing relatively good relations with the Native Americans, alkaline soil, a drought, squabbling among the Mormons, and an anticipated war between the Mormons of Utah and federal troops caused most of the settlers to leave the valley in 1857. Their buildings and irrigation systems remained, assisting the next wave of immigrants to the valley.[9]

Non-Mormon ranchers and merchants followed, making their mark on the area. One of the most important was Octavius Decatur "O. D." Gass, who, with partners, established a ranch where the Mormon missionaries had earlier constructed their fort. Gass built a flat-roofed adobe house within the Mormon fort's ruins, reputedly using an adobe fort wall for one of his buildings. During the 1870s, Gass bought out his partners and supported his family by raising crops, tending cattle, and selling fresh meat, produce, and homemade wine to local miners and emigrants on the Spanish Trail.[10]

Conrad Kiel, a native of Pennsylvania and one of Gass's friends, may have moved to the Las Vegas area at his prompting. For a time, Kiel operated a sawmill on Mount Charleston, giving his name to Kyle Canyon (reflecting a misspelling of his name). Kiel's ranch in the Las Vegas Valley lay about one and a half miles north of Gass's ranch on the site where the Mormon missionaries had earlier established what they called an Indian farm. Kiel's development incorporated the remnants of the earlier Mormon settlement. According to local tradition, their legacy included the rudimentary adobe structure that survived into the twenty-first century, making it a contender for the title of oldest existing building in the state.[11]

Unfortunately, time has obscured verifiable history. Although it is true that adobe was one of the early Mormon settlers' favorite building materials, it may not be possible to determine when the building was actually constructed. There are, in fact, indications that it may be much younger than previously thought. Architectural historian Jim Steely points out that the use of milled boards and the presence of a gabled roof, when earlier adobe structures, such as those built by Gass, had flat roofs, suggest the Kiel adobe may date to a period shortly after the turn of the twentieth century. That the crumbling building became the focus of folklore underscores the value people place on remnants of the earliest settlement. Legend is often more powerful than fact. Except for the bragging rights of declaring it as one of the oldest buildings in the state, it matters little whether the Mormons, Gass, Kiel, or later farmers built the structure.[12]

The subsequent history of Kiel Ranch is more easily verified. Given his friendship with Gass, it is likely that Kiel was troubled when Archibald Stewart, a wealthy rancher from Pioche, foreclosed on Gass's property mortgage in 1881. When Stewart died in a gunfight at Kiel's ranch in 1884 while Kiel was away, Kiel expressed little sympathy about the incident to newly widowed Helen Stewart.[13]

The 1884 killing is emblematic of Kiel Ranch's history. Even before Stewart died at the ranch, it had acquired an unsavory reputation as a sanctuary for gunslingers and other ne'er-do-wells. Stewart's death furthered this perception, as did a second tragedy at the ranch. In 1900, the late Conrad Kiel's two sons were found shot dead at the ranch. The coroner ruled the deaths a murder-suicide. Forensic analysis performed during the 1990s by the Anthropology Department of the University of Nevada–Las Vegas challenged this conclusion and suggested, instead, that both of Kiel's sons had been murdered by an unknown party, although suspicion rests with one of Helen Stewart's own sons. The story of violent deaths perpetuated the ranch's reputation into the twentieth century.

After the tragedy of 1900, the Kiel family sold their land to the Utah, Nevada, and California Railroad Company, owned by copper king Senator William Clark of Montana. Although the railroad needed the land principally for its right-of-way and did little to improve its acquisition, better days were in store for the old ranch. In 1911, John S. Park, manager of the First State Bank, acquired the property and turned it into one of the valley's more glamorous gathering places and successful bulk food producers. He constructed a mansion, known as the "White House," where he hosted lavish parties, often featuring cultured entertainment. During this period Kiel Ranch assumed the appearance that would be familiar to southern Nevadans for decades. Numerous simple wooden outbuildings and the aging small adobe structure, now probably a cool-storage pantry for produce, were scattered among mature trees, but it was the ranch's White House that attracted most of the attention. The imposing Crafts-man structure with clapboard siding and a pillar-supported porch domi-nated the complex. During the 1920s, Edward Taylor assumed control of Kiel Ranch, and in 1939, he leased it to Edwin Losee for a new phase of stewardship. As the "Boulderado Dude Ranch," land that Mormons once cultivated now catered to the Las Vegas Valley's divorce trade.

In the 1960s, the Kiel Ranch, along with its old adobe structure and the White House, fell into the hands of developers, threatening its survival. In 1974, however, the North Las Vegas Bicentennial Committee purchased the venerable property partly with federal funds and turned it over to the City of North Las Vegas for use as a regional park. The city, claiming it needed to raise funds to develop the site, sold much of the acreage for warehousing and light industry. The sale left the standing buildings and the original spring on a shrinking six-acre island of open space with a declining ability to serve the public.

In 1991, the city began raising funds to restore the remaining struc-tures, securing support from the Commission for Cultural Affairs. Almost immediately, disaster again befell the ill-fated ranch when an arsonist torched the White House, coincidentally within weeks of the award of the commission grant. After these setbacks, only a small bit of the original complex remained, and few held out hope for a park at that location.

Through all of this, the humble adobe building survived. As a work of architecture, it exhibited a modest approach to the problem of secur-ing shelter. Stacked sun-dried bricks formed four walls and supported a sturdy roof, serving the immediate needs of those seeking protection from the elements. Long-term survival may have been hard to imagine. Nevertheless, this building outlasted its neighbors as well as all expec-tations. Unfortunately, even a tenacious building cannot thwart grav-ity forever. While the city erected a barnlike shelter above the adobe and searched for ways to preserve the remarkable artifact, one of its walls collapsed. As this rare survivor of the nineteenth century stumbles into a new millennium, its future remains uncertain. It has yet to achieve the 1970s Bicentennial Committee's vision of becoming a cultural center or the intent of the grants from the state Commission for Cultural Affairs, but where there is survival, hope lingers.

FOREMAN-ROBERTS HOUSE

The rudimentary nature of the adobe structure, which so clearly illustrates the earliest history of southern Nevada, contrasts with the Foreman-Roberts House in Carson City. This building clearly dates to the territorial period, but like the Kiel Ranch adobe, its specific origin became a matter of folklore. For decades, local tradition maintained that what eventually became known as the Roberts House was built in 1859. Research has demonstrated the building in fact dates to 1863 during the Nevada—not the Utah—territorial period. In addition, logic challenges the widely held belief that the house was transported on the Virginia and Truckee (V&T) Railroad. The narrow right-of-way would not have accommodated the house, which was more likely moved from Washoe Valley to Carson City by wagon. The manner in which the Foreman-Roberts House, like the Kiel Ranch adobe, became part of oral tradition underscores both the enthusiasm of later generations who revered early remnants and the problems inherent in researching the real stories of older buildings.[14]

In spite of the folklore and its deviation from fact, it is possible to understand much of the first settlement history of these regions. Paralleling the first settlement patterns of Euro-Americans in southern Nevada, Mormons were attracted to the valleys along the eastern slope of the Sierra Nevada. They established farms and sold supplies to emigrants as the latter passed through Nevada on their way to and from California. The first of the northern towns to emerge was Mormon Station, now called Genoa, founded in 1851. The followers of the Church of Jesus Christ of Latter-day Saints also built farms and small communities along the well-watered strip of land lying at the eastern base of the Sierra.

Washoe Valley, to the north of Mormon Station, was particularly

Carson City's Foreman-Roberts House is an outstanding example of Gothic
Revival architecture, in this case dating to the state's territorial period.

attractive because mountain creeks watered its broad expanse of flat,
arable acreage before emptying into Washoe Lake. The lure of water
attracted Mormon farmers here as it had in the Las Vegas Valley. Unlike
those who went south, however, the first settlers to develop the eastern
slope of the Sierra were not all of one faith. "Gentiles," as the Mormons
called nonbelievers, also played a role in the valleys. When Brigham Young
called his followers back to Utah in 1857 because of the threat of war with
federal troops, the remaining Gentiles gladly claimed abandoned Mormon farms.[15]

Scattered placer miners in the region had always provided a small market for Washoe Valley produce, but a major gold and silver strike in 1859,
founding the nearby Comstock Mining District, enhanced the valley's eco-

nomic opportunities. Solomon W. Foreman constructed a home there in 1863, no doubt in response to its thriving economy. It was a good choice. In addition to having the agricultural market enhanced by the Comstock's burgeoning population, mine owners began building mills in Washoe Valley. Further, with the organization of the Nevada Territory in 1861, Washoe City became the seat of government for the newly formed Washoe County, and the subsequent economic benefits of tax revenues began flowing into the valley.

Unfortunately, prosperity in the valley was fleeting. The transcontinental railroad was completed in 1868, and Reno, to the north of Washoe Valley, grew from a small settlement into a major transportation hub. Coincidentally, the Virginia and Truckee Railroad completed its line from Carson City to Virginia City in 1869, making it cheaper to haul ore from the Comstock to mills on the Carson River. Teamsters hauling ore from Virginia City's mines over the Virginia Range down to Washoe Valley were now a thing of the past. In 1872, the Nevada legislature moved the seat of Washoe County government to Reno, and Washoe City lost another source of revenue.

With these changes, Washoe Valley resumed its role as a sleepy home to agriculture, a place where prosperity was counted by heads of cattle rather than by tons of processed ore or the number of its businesses. Faced with this economic decline, James Doan Roberts, who had acquired Foreman's house in 1867, moved the structure in 1873 to the corner of Corbett and Carson streets in Carson City.

The Foreman-Roberts House is one of Nevada's better examples of Gothic Revival architecture. That style, popular in the United States at the time, was a formal approach to design intended to demonstrate the sophistication and respectability of a prosperous middle class. Its appearance on the Nevada landscape indicated that the frontier was passing on the eastern slope of the Sierra with a speed unprecedented in other parts of the country. Nevada was being integrated virtually overnight into the industrial society of nineteenth-century America. Another prominent

example of this style is the privately owned Winters Ranch at the north end
of Washoe Valley, which slightly predates the Foreman-Roberts House.
With grand Gothic windows and gables, both houses express the prosperity of the valley at the time.[16] After sheltering the Roberts family for
decades, the house ceased to be a home. A local group assumed ownership
of the real estate and has operated the property as a museum ever since.

GENOA COURTHOUSE

The courthouse in Genoa is a rare example of monumental architecture from the territorial period in Nevada. Formally known as Mormon
Station, Genoa began as a farming community and trading post nestled
on the eastern slope of the Sierra Nevada along the overland route linking
Carson Valley to California's Central Valley. The settlement became the
seat of Utah Territory's Carson County in 1854. After Orson Hyde surveyed
the town in 1855, it acquired the name Genoa, honoring the birthplace of
Columbus. With the organization of the Nevada Territory in 1861, Genoa
became the seat of Douglas County.[17]

In 1864, the territorial legislature allowed Douglas County to tax property owners for the construction of a courthouse. The county hired T. J.
Furbee, a local mining superintendent, to design a two-story brick structure. His plan called for a substantial courthouse of modest scale. Like
many vernacular-style buildings of the territorial period, it combined
diverse architectural elements in ways that the builder and the community
saw as aesthetically pleasing.[18]

The courthouse opened in 1865, shortly after Nevada gained statehood,
but the structure exhibits the sort of modest approach to monumental
architecture that corresponds to its territorial roots. The courthouse has
a courtroom on its second floor and a jail—little more than an iron box—
in the rear of its first floor. The building's brick facade is truly its proudest
feature. Centrally placed doors with sidelights and transoms on the main
and second floors, the building's surrounding windows, and a dentil cornice work together to lend a classical air to the vernacular building.

The courthouse in Genoa is an early example of monumental construction. Designed before Nevada became a state, the structure survives as home to a local museum.

By the time the courthouse was complete, other communities were already challenging Genoa's privileged position along the trade routes linking Nevada to California. With the discovery of the Comstock in 1859, Carson City emerged as the larger of the valley towns. After the Central Pacific Railroad established Reno in 1868 as the site of a transcontinental railroad depot, that town also eclipsed Genoa. In addition, two disasters devastated Genoa. In 1882, an avalanche roared down the steep slope to the community's west and buried much of the place. Three decades later, in 1910, an indigent set a fire that destroyed most of the town and gutted the courthouse, yet Furbee's sturdy structure remained standing. The county repaired the facility and then five years later decided to move its seat to Minden, indicating the end of an era in Douglas County. Genoa would survive, however, and its courthouse served until 1956 as a school. In 1969, it became a museum, and as such it continues to stand as a reminder of the final days of the territorial period.[19]

TOGETHER, the Kiel Ranch adobe, the Foreman-Roberts House, and the Genoa Courthouse give a hint of life in the 1850s and early 1860s. The adobe is a crude structure, which, with a minimal amount of effort, offered shelter from the heat, wind, and rare desert rainstorms. It was the sort of building that captures a sense of the desperate, immediate needs of people who arrived in a harsh environment and planned to stay. Within the bricks of the Kiel Ranch adobe are the hopes and aspirations of those who built it and of everyone who followed them into the Las Vegas Valley, hoping to make it their home.

The Foreman-Roberts House represents a second early phase of Nevada architecture. It is not a first-settlement building. Whereas the crude log cabin at the foot of forested mountains had been the rule in northwestern Nevada only a few years before, that early period of settlement already seemed like ancient history when Solomon Foreman built his home in Washoe Valley in 1863. Times changed rapidly, and more people were arriving. The Foreman-Roberts House represents an attempt to introduce a level of sophistication into Nevada's nineteenth-century architecture. Its detailed woodwork and recognizable style testify to how people sought to establish a reputable home during the second phase of settlement. The house was humble by eastern cosmopolitan standards, but it was a real step up for Nevada.

The courthouse in Genoa was one of the earliest attempts in the territory to construct a monumental building. At best, however, the region's population was limited, and funding grand public facilities was a low priority. Douglas County did the best it could, just as settlers had done with adobe shelters in southern Nevada and the Foreman-Roberts House.

The architecture of these three buildings reached as far as possible for the time. Ultimately, the Genoa Courthouse showed that the territory's seemingly inherent limits could be stretched to a remarkable degree. Its architecture exhibits its own mixture of simplicity and grandeur. In spite of limited financial resources, Nevada was emerging as a place of substance, and its early structures would increasingly reflect that fact.

Kiel Ranch, the Foreman-Roberts House, and the Genoa Courthouse tell a fascinating tale of early settlers scraping together an existence and inventing bold new ways of life in an austere environment that offered a meek chance to survive. As captivating as the stories of these early buildings are, they are in fact little more than sideshows when considering the gold and silver strikes that changed the direction of the region's history and captured international attention during the 1860s and 1870s. Nineteenth-century Nevada would be renowned for its mining, not for its agriculture or its overland commerce, which were the economic foundations of the early communities that emerged around Las Vegas Springs, in Washoe Valley, and in Genoa.

2 A State of International Fame

Had it not been for the pivotal events of 1859, the Kiel Ranch adobe, the Foreman-Roberts House, and the Genoa Courthouse would have been harbingers of the region's future economic development, foretelling of growth in its agricultural and transportation industries. Nevada's fate, however, would be shaped by its mineral wealth. The exploitation of its rich ore deposits would dominate the state's history and indelibly mark its emergent culture. Early prospectors arriving in the 1850s began to change the character of the region. Then, in January and June 1859, placer miners discovered rich outcroppings of gold and silver ore in a mountain range lying east of the Sierra. Several hundred men and women established the Comstock Mining District and founded Virginia City, Gold Hill, and Silver City. From these rudimentary beginnings, urban life would emerge almost overnight.[1]

The Comstock's incredible wealth achieved international fame and transformed Nevada into a land where the lucky could become millionaires. Thousands of hardy souls from diverse lands would eventually traverse every mountain in the region and found many other mining districts, but none would be as fabulous as the Comstock. Seeking to exploit the West's mineral resources, they scattered mining towns across its land-scape, and civilization flickered in desert wastes.

The economic achievements of these pioneers are easily counted in the thousands of tons of gold and silver they extracted from the earth. These engineering accomplishments are testified to by the mining technolo-gies they invented, which would influence the industry for another fifty years. Nevertheless, as the first generation of miners understood, sim-ply surviving in Nevada's harsh environments was itself a triumph. The eastern slope of the Sierra contrasted markedly with its lush, well-watered western counterpart, home of the California Gold Rush. Nevada's boom-towns inhabited arid mountains and desert expanses, and the people who persisted there needed to figure out how to make these places work. They devised new approaches to erecting infrastructure that brought water, food, and materials to the remote outback. Although historians often note that the Comstock's massive outpouring of gold and silver destabilized the international monetary system and contributed to the economic chaos of the 1870s, scholars frequently overlook the equally influential pattern of urban development pioneered by innovative communities in what would become Nevada, mining camps imitated everywhere from Colorado and Montana to South Africa and Australia.

Because of mining's boom-and-bust cycle, hundreds of buildings from this period have fallen into heaps in Nevada's ghost towns, leav-ing only archaeological shadows while many that still stand survive as neglected orphans. These remnants of Nevada's nineteenth-century glory days haunt its windswept mountains and desert wastes, adding character to the region. Still, the story of Nevada mining began with the Comstock, and most of its communities avoided ghost town status. Today, the Vir-ginia City Landmark District includes roughly fourteen thousand acres and more than five hundred historic structures. Moreover, Dayton, at the southern end of the Comstock, boasts a significant commercial and resi-dential corridor that is often ignored in spite of its importance to the early settlement of the region.

DAYTON SCHOOLHOUSE

Tradition maintains that as early as 1848, Mexican miners may have discovered gold where a creek flowed from Gold Canyon into the Carson River. Nevertheless, Abner Blackburn, a miner on his way to California in 1849, is credited with the first clearly documented gold strike in the area. By the spring of 1851, roughly two hundred miners, many erstwhile forty-niners, had settled in the region and begun working sandbars laden with gold dust and an occasional nugget. This early influx has led some historians to conclude that Dayton rather than the Mormon colony at Genoa was Nevada's first settlement.[2]

Shortly after the discovery of placer gold, Spafford Hall founded a trad-

The stone schoolhouse in Dayton dates to 1865 and is one of the oldest of its kind in the state.

ing post in Gold Canyon, and a small community formed around it. During the 1850s, placer miners worked claims and purchased supplies from Hall's establishment. In 1856, a group of Chinese laborers, originally brought into the area to dig a ditch, settled on the edge of the community and also began placer mining along the creek. Because of these Asian residents, the community at the mouth of Gold Canyon was sometimes called Chinatown. After prospectors working on the mountain above the Carson River discovered the Comstock Lode in 1859, Dayton residents began supporting themselves by supplying goods and services to the region's mining interests. In 1861, the town took the name Dayton, in honor of the community's surveyor.[3]

Dayton, like many other mining towns, defied demographic stereotypes by attracting increasing numbers of women. The early presence of families required schools, and Dayton's 1865 schoolhouse represents the sort of substantial stone building that a maturing community would erect. For many Nevada settlements, the mid-1860s were far too early to consider establishing a permanent home for education, but Dayton's founding in the 1850s made it just the place to erect the state's oldest surviving masonry school. Of course, residents often romanticize their cherished earliest schools as being the oldest in their states, and historians are often skeptical about such claims. Nevertheless, it appears that the revered Dayton structure is older than most other schools in Nevada, and it has survived longer than any other masonry school in the state. Unquestionably, it housed students for an extraordinary number of years, serving Dayton's local children until 1959. After that, it became a senior center. In 1993, the Dayton Historic Society began restoring the schoolhouse as a local museum, a capacity that it fulfills to this day.[4]

The well-constructed Dayton schoolhouse exhibits a sophisticated sense of design, employing the Greek Revival–architectural style that lent mid-nineteenth-century public buildings a degree of classical finesse. Various elements in the Dayton facility—the lintels over its windows, its front gable pediment with the eave returns, and its overall symmetry—

refer to Greek architecture. Still, its quoins—the finished stone treatment on its corners—are more at home with other architectural styles. Because of its mixed motifs and early date of construction, it is likely that this building was not architect designed. Nevertheless, even with its vernacular origins, its substantial masonry provided Dayton's children with an urbane home for education for nearly a century.

VIRGINIA CITY'S FIRE MUSEUM

Whereas Dayton is the oldest of the Comstock towns, other settlements grew up in the mining district in the wake of its great mineral strikes. The most important of these were Virginia City and Gold Hill, historic communities boasting more than their share of early building. Virginia City's Fire Museum presents an attractive redbrick single-story facade dating to the early 1860s. Although this date places the resource within the territorial period, like those discussed in chapter 1, this structure was tied to the mining industry and the future of Nevada. Originally serving as a grocery store and for a time as a saloon, the structure's false front made it typical of the many commercial buildings along Virginia City's main street.[5]

The use of brick signals that this is a second-phase addition to the community. The first settlers on the slopes of Mount Davidson lived and worked in tents or simple wooden structures. Although modest, the structure's simple brick edifice reveals that its builders wanted to underscore its permanence and respectability. Indeed, the creative use of brick to demarcate details, including a cornice with dentils and the subtle arches over its doorways and windows, makes for a stylish presentation.

In 1934, the community drafted the versatile building for use as a firehouse. Firemen removed one of the brick columns to open a single bay wide enough for vehicles, but otherwise much of the historic fabric remained. The building served as a firehouse until 1962, when Virginia City's Fire Department moved to new quarters. In 1979, Liberty Engine Company No. 1 converted the building into a volunteer-run museum.[6]

The history of firefighting on the Comstock is filled with tales of des-

Now serving as Virginia City's Fire Museum, the territorial-era building originally served as a grocery store.

perate acts of bravery to save lives and property, making the building a fine venue to celebrate the community's heroic past. Over the years, Liberty Engine Company No. 1 has restored numerous pieces of equipment and artifacts associated with the various fire departments of Virginia City and Gold Hill. Today, the Fire Museum continues to bring life to the history of the Comstock's fires and those who struggled against them.

GOLD HILL DEPOT

Gold Hill's depot is among a handful of surviving buildings associated with one of the world's most famous short line railroads. The Virginia and Truckee Railroad, the famed V&T, began in 1869 as a route from Carson City to Gold Hill. By 1872, the line extended from Virginia City to Reno and connected with the transcontinental railroad, the quintessential symbol of America's technological achievements during the expansive era of the second Industrial Revolution.

Paralleling the monopolistic tendencies of the Gilded Age, William Sharon and the Bank of California sought to control all aspects of Comstock mining. After purchasing the richest claims on the lode, Sharon built the V&T and established mills for crushing ore along its Carson River route.[7] The railroad contributed to the "Bank Crowd's" vertical integration of the mining district, consolidating the transport of ore to mills, bullion to the U.S. Mint in Carson City, and supplies back to the towns of the Comstock. Although the V&T originated as part of the bank's monopoly, it outlived the control of the financial institution. By establishing connections between the Comstock and Nevada's western valleys, the railroad ultimately benefited all segments of western Nevada's commercial and social life.

Because the line initially ended in Gold Hill, its depot was the first to receive passengers on the newly inaugurated service. The core component of the building was a large construction shed moved to Gold Hill when the railroad first arrived in 1869. Modifications over the years transformed it into a classic nineteenth-century railroad depot with knee brace–supported eaves, a platform, a freight room, and amenities such as a ticket office, sitting room, and ladies' parlor.

After the railroad finally ceased to serve Gold Hill and Virginia City in 1938, the owners gave the depot to Storey County for use as a museum and as a monument to the role the V&T played in Nevada's early mining history. In 1974, the Carson City Railroad Association followed by the Comstock Historical Railroad Foundation and then the Gold Hill Historical Society began restoration work. Its future secured, the depot stands ready to serve a steadily expanding and rejuvenated Virginia and Truckee Railroad. With its line extending to Mound House and eventually to Carson City, the railroad promises to continue growing as a major tourist attraction. The depot, one of the oldest of the V&T relics, will function as it once did when the Comstock's first trains pulled into Gold Hill. As Nevadans reconstruct one of the engineering marvels of the nineteenth century, they piece together the resources that are available to them, just as their enterprising predecessors had cobbled together the original V&T depot in Gold Hill in the 1860s.

ST. MARY'S ART CENTER

Society and culture reached its nineteenth-century height on the Comstock during the 1870s, and this fact is reflected in the refinement of its architecture. One of the most imposing structures surviving from this era is the building that today houses the St. Mary's Art Center. In 1873, the estate of Gen. Jacob Van Bokkelin, recently killed in a dynamite explosion,

St. Mary Louise Hospital dominated the valley below Virginia City after its construction in the 1870s. A grove of trees recalls a time when it was a peaceful retreat for healing the sick.

offered his Virginia City beer garden for sale. Mary Louise Mackay, wife of Bonanza king John Mackay, saw the tree-shaded site downhill from the community as perfect for a private hospital. She purchased the land and gave it to the Daughters of Charity, who operated a school and orphanage in town. Three years later they opened St. Mary Louise Hospital.[8] The four-story brick building exhibits formal architectural details that communicate its institutional nature. A large porch framed by Doric columns and a setting employing six acres of well-landscaped grounds lend the entire complex the feel of a grand estate.

The hospital featured thirty-six rooms and two kitchens. It quickly became the community's preferred medical establishment, eclipsing the county hospital and various small private facilities. The Daughters of Charity lived on the top floor, which included a padded cell with bars on the windows for unstable guests needing special accommodations. Although the Daughters left Virginia City in 1897, the hospital continued to serve Virginia City and its surrounding areas until the 1940s, when it closed and reverted to Storey County.

In 1964, community leaders persuaded Father Paul Meinecke to assume control of the structure. Inspired by Louise Curran, a local artist, Father Meinecke decided to convert the hospital into an arts center. By the spring of 1964, the old hospital, now rechristened St. Mary's Art Center, opened, and Curran served as its first director.[9]

St. Mary Louise Hospital is a grand establishment, symbolizing a mining community at the height of bonanza. It testifies to the mining town's interest in providing people with the best possible health care. At the same time, its dignified design and handsome landscaping attest to the refined taste prevalent in nineteenth-century Virginia City. The imposing structure dominates the view to the east from the center of town, and its beautiful grounds still echo the original setting.

FOURTH WARD SCHOOL

No structure on the Comstock or perhaps even in the state provides more insight into the ideals and aspirations of Nevada's nineteenth-century mining frontier than Virginia City's Fourth Ward School. Built in 1876 as the community's centennial school, the four-story building was designed to house one thousand students from the city's fourth political subdivision. Opening to public acclaim in 1877, it featured such forward-looking accoutrements as central heating, flush toilets, running water for drinking fountains, and a large multipurpose room with pocket doors for conversion into classrooms. C. M. Bennett, a local architect, drew on the French Second Empire–architectural style to give the building an imposing, sophisticated look, including its mansard roof. At least one period pattern book published plans nearly identical to those used for the Fourth Ward, so Bennett probably drew on such a source. Underscoring the importance of the Fourth Ward School to the people of Virginia City, the *Territorial Enterprise* opined, "If it is our pride today, the time is not too distant when it will [also] be our glory. . . . [O]ur free schools are justly regarded as the bulwarks of our nation."[10]

Like numerous American cities of the time, the Comstock mining community was devoted to the idea of giving children a comprehensive education. By 1865, in fact, twelve public schools operated in Storey County, and five years later, 85 percent of the district's children were enrolled. Although the Comstock boasted a profusion of public schools when it was

Opened in 1877, the four-story Fourth Ward School dominated the southern end of town. Built for more than one thousand students, the building is now home to a local museum.

at its height, none represented the community's social and cultural ideals more than Virginia City's Fourth Ward School.[11]

For sixty years the Fourth Ward School served the children of Storey County. Unfortunately, as the great Comstock mines began to fail in the 1880s, the community also declined. In 1936, Virginia City was forced to close the school, moving the students to a new federally funded building in the center of town. Though the Fourth Ward School stood vacant for five decades, it was not forgotten by those who had been educated within its walls, and due perhaps to their reminiscences, the building remained an important part of Virginia City's heritage. Indeed, a twenty-five-year restoration project beginning in 1983 and the opening of the facility as a museum in 1986 contributed to a resurgence of art and culture on the Comstock.

ST. AUGUSTINE'S CATHOLIC CHURCH

The extraordinary discoveries on the Comstock stimulated a wave of gold and silver exploration in the lands lying west of the Great Salt Lake and east of the Sierra Nevada in the 1860s and 1870s. "Old sourdoughs," as prospectors of the time were known, fanned out across this mountainous terrain, making new discoveries and fueling legends of Nevada's fabulous mineral wealth. In 1862, William Talcott contributed to local lore when he located silver ore in Pony Canyon, a pass through central Nevada's Toiyabe Mountains in the Reese River region. The strike attracted newcomers who founded the town of Clifton below the new claims. David Buel then platted Austin up the canyon, naming his town for his partner, Alvah Austin. The community boomed the following year. During a temporary decline in gold and silver production on the Comstock, a momentarily depressed Virginia City even contributed its International Hotel to an ascending Austin, with enterprising businessmen moving the substantial building 170 miles before planting it in its new home. The 1862 "Rush to Reese River" sparked the creation of Lander County by the Nevada legislature, and in 1863, Austin became its seat of government.

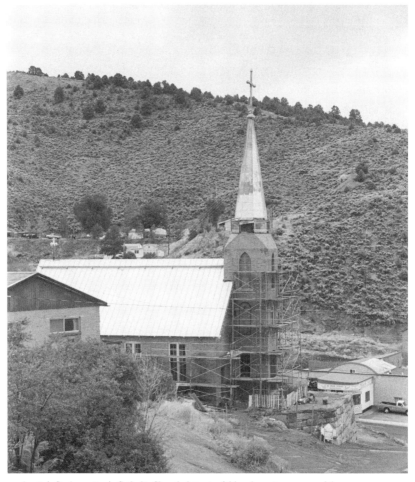

Austin's St. Augustine's Catholic Church dates to 1866 and survives as one of the more impressive buildings in town.

Austin incorporated as a city in 1864. The following year, the Manhattan Silver Mining Company began purchasing mines and mills, nearly monopolizing the local industry. Productivity, though consistent, remained modest. The strike at Austin was noteworthy, but it could not compete with the resumed, tremendous outpouring of riches from the Comstock. Nevertheless, Austin served as a springboard for exploration and exploitation of central Nevada's mineral resources, and it established a network of communication, commerce, and finance that encouraged the growth of Hamilton and Treasure Hill, Eureka, Belmont, Tuscarora, and many other mining towns.

By 1890, Austin's mines were in a steep decline, and the town's population dwindled to a little more than one thousand. Limited mining continued in the area, however, into the twentieth century. A 1979 election transferred the county seat to Battle Mountain, stripping Austin of one of its remaining industries. Today, the Austin Historic District on Highway 50 survives as a reminder of one of the nineteenth century's great centers of mining, but its economy and size are limited.[12]

Austin's St. Augustine's Catholic Church was built in 1866 when the community was first establishing itself. The brick Gothic church stands on a stone foundation. It features a tall front tower, supporting an octagonal spire that dominates the town. An ornate entrance features round concrete steps. Pairs of multipane windows illuminate the sides of the building, with a small ocular opening at the rear. Inside, five flat segments form a barrel-like vault, spanning a space that includes a choir loft featuring a nineteenth-century Henry Kilgen organ with Gothic details. Religious murals date to about 1940.

Although western mining towns often boasted that they were irreligious, violent places, the erection of a church was usually a welcomed benchmark, demonstrating permanence and an ascending quality of life. Austin's Catholic church is a formidable structure, built to last and to make a powerful statement. It affirms the spiritual commitment that sustained many mining families confronted with the whims of fortune, characteristic of life in Nevada's boomtowns. Its imposing Gothic edifice, recalling an earlier spiritual age, has dominated the town since its completion. As the community dwindled in the late twentieth century, so did the parish. Eventually, far too few people were left to support the mighty old edifice. In 2004, the Catholic diocese transferred St. Augustine's Church to a nonprofit organization with the condition that when a priest is in town, the building resumes its original function, but at other times it serves the community in a wide variety of cultural capacities.

TUSCARORA SOCIETY HALL

As prospectors dispersed from Austin, several of them discovered rich placer sands located in what is now Elko County. In 1867, shortly after the Civil War, one of the miners working northeast of Austin called the place where he was finding gold "Tuscarora" to honor a Union gunboat on which he had served. Underground mineral deposits attracted some attention, but surface placer mining was the primary focus. Prosperity remained elusive until Chinese workers, recently discharged from the completed transcontinental railroad, began arriving in 1869. They purchased placer claims and turned them to profit.

Local Euro-Americans focused their attention on Tuscarora's underground mines, which were occasionally prosperous, especially from 1877 to 1880 and from 1887 to 1892. At its height, the town grew to a population of roughly three thousand, attracting people from depressed mining districts in other parts of the region. The thriving town held considerable promise until mining depleted the ore bodies, and Tuscarora's population began to decline dramatically beginning in the late 1890s.

The community built the Tuscarora Society Hall in 1877, when the town was at its height. Constructed of stone quarried from local pits, the lower floor served as a saloon, while its upper level housed Tuscarora's diverse secret societies, including the Free and Accepted Masons, Independent Order of Odd Fellows, Knights of Pythias, Pythian Sisters, and Ancient Order of United Working Men. The structure served as a Masonic lodge for decades, but in the 1950s the local fraternal chapter disbanded. The old stone structure still functioned as a saloon and meeting place for community events and weddings. It became known as the Tuscarora Tavern, but after a number of years, it fell into disuse because it needed extensive repairs.

In 2001, the town's two dozen permanent residents, its seasonal

Built in 1877, the Tuscarora Society Hall served a number of fraternal organizations during the nineteenth century.

inhabitants, and the ranchers of Independence Valley purchased the structure and donated it to Elko County, hoping it could serve them once again. As the Friends of Tuscarora complete the structure's rehabilitation, the group is using the facility as a community center, museum, and historical resource center. Functioning in this capacity, it disseminates information to the community's visitors, focusing on Tuscarora's early mining history and the role it played in the development of northeastern Nevada. Equally as important, the refurbished social center serves as a reminder of the rich fraternal life that was a cornerstone of nineteenth-century mining communities. Functioning as tiny outposts of civilization, seemingly dwarfed by the grandeur of Nevada's foreboding landscapes, the sociability characteristic of boomtowns ameliorated the sense of loneliness often plaguing the frontier.

LINCOLN COUNTY COURTHOUSE

The mountain town of Pioche, near the eastern border of the state, proved to be one of the more prosperous and long lived of Nevada's mining camps. It emerged after the discoveries on the Comstock and around the time Austin flourished in the late 1860s. In the wake of the mining rush to the area, the 1871 Nevada legislature shifted the seat of Lincoln County government from Hiko to Pioche. Within a year, the community erected a monumental two-story brick courthouse, a clear demonstration of Pioche's aspirations for stability.

T. Dimmock and Thomas Keefe designed the Italianate-style structure with fine details crafted in brick and sidewalls of stone. The expert use of brick separates bays for windows and the doorway and creates a cornice with dentils and a false front. A graceful fanlight above the main entrance finds an echo in the gentle curve of a transom above the second-story door to a balcony. These details distinguish the building as one of the more elegant architectural creations of early Nevada. They also testify to the refinement of taste exhibited by at least some in a mining camp that would acquire the reputation of being one of the wildest in the state's history.

More consistent, perhaps, with the community's legendary reputation is the fact that the Lincoln County Courthouse would become famous for something other than its style. The building is known, in fact, as the "million-dollar courthouse." The county originally awarded Edward Donahue a $16,400 contract for its construction. The addition of a jail added roughly $10,000 to the project, while changes to the contract and adjustments in financing drove the price of the building up to $75,000 by its opening.

The county was slow to repay the balance, which it refinanced several times, further increasing the cost. The courthouse debt became an important issue in 1909 when Clark County broke away from Lincoln County. The residents of the new southern county did not wish to bear the burden of Pioche's financial mismanagement, but they finally assumed a share of the liability, paying nearly a half-million dollars as the price of inde-

Lincoln County opened its Pioche courthouse in 1872. Officials failed to properly finance the construction of the facility, which eventually cost the local government nearly a million dollars.

pendence. When Lincoln County's courthouse debt was finally retired in 1938, it was said to be nearly a million dollars, inspiring the building's nickname. Historian and Lincoln County native James W. Hulse estimates that the actual cost was closer to $800,000, but the larger figure had a better ring and has won the facility considerable fame, if not infamy.[13]

In 1938, Lincoln County opened a more modest courthouse, employing Art Deco design. The original public facility then served as a meeting room and polling place, but the structure's condition deteriorated, eventually making it unusable. Faced with the possibility of having the building demolished or even moved to the Las Vegas Strip as an attraction, a local constituency organized to save the courthouse. With funding from the State Historic Preservation Office, Lincoln County saved the old building and in 1981 reopened it as a local museum. Subsequent grants have extended its life and continued its legend into a new century.

The grand Lincoln County building is the epitome of what a nineteenth-century mining-town courthouse should look like. It aspires to achieve a monumental, permanent presence, but its design is simple and direct, if not rugged. In contrast, the delicate fanlight above the main entrance speaks to a softening of a civil presence in a mining boomtown proud of the perception that it had a violent, rough-and-tumble origin.

MINERAL COUNTY COURTHOUSE

The Mineral County Courthouse is yet another example of how nineteenth-century Nevadans attempted to demonstrate that the mining frontier could be a stable, permanent place. Hawthorne is one of Nevada's more durable communities. It began as a railroad town associated with the Carson and Colorado Railroad, and its principal function was to serve as a distribution center for mining in the region. William M. Sharon and Darius O. Mills, founders of the Virginia and Truckee Railroad, hoped to encourage mineral exploitation and production to the south along the eastern slope of the Sierra Nevada. In 1881, they established a line that connected with the V&T at Mound House to the southern tip of Walker Lake. They set up a division point there and called it Hawthorne.[14]

Hawthorne's Mineral County Courthouse dates to 1883. Its fate is yet to be determined.

Mining near Hawthorne did not prove as lucrative as Sharon and Mills hoped, but the town they established endured, supported in part by ranches and farms huddled around Walker Lake. Because Aurora, the seat of Esmeralda County, had long been in a decline, Hawthorne inherited the reins of government, and the county commissioners built a courthouse there in 1883. The two-story brick Italianate building features a bracketed cornice and a peculiar five-sided entry porch with wooden columns and a balustrade. Pedimented gables above the cornice line give the building a classical air and invest it with the dignity and gravity that community leaders of the time deemed appropriate for their governmental structures.[15]

Hawthorne lost the seat of Esmeralda County to the booming town of Goldfield in 1907. Yet simply by surviving a little longer, Hawthorne became a county seat again, in 1911, when the Nevada legislature created Mineral County. Its courthouse subsequently is the only Nevada building to serve in that capacity for two counties.[16]

While the Hawthorne courthouse was still serving as the county seat of Esmeralda County, one of Nevada's most notorious court cases was decided within its walls. In the spring of 1907, two labor organizers, Morris "Morrie" Preston and Joseph William Smith, were tried in the courthouse for the murder of John Silva, a Goldfield restaurant owner. Although there was ample evidence indicating Preston had shot Silva in self-defense, Preston was found guilty of murder and Smith was convicted of manslaughter. Because their trial occurred at the height of a labor dispute in Goldfield and antiunion sentiment was running high, the two men were judged unfairly. In fact, the affront to justice represented by their conviction made their trial a cause célèbre in the nation's labor circles. The following year, the Socialist Labor Party nominated Preston for president of the United States. Although both men had received lengthy sentences for the crime, the Nevada Parole Board, recognizing the injustices associated with the case, released them earlier than had originally been anticipated. Years later, the Nevada Pardons Board granted them posthumous pardons for the crime.[17]

In 1929, Hawthorne gained a new sort of prominence when the United States Navy established its principal ammunitions depot there. As a result, hundreds of people poured into the region, seeking employment at the depot and turning the community, once again, into a boomtown. The role the federal government played in expanding the community is reminiscent of the escalating role that Washington, D.C., played in the lives of many communities across the nation during the Great Depression and the middle decades of the twentieth century. When the munitions depot was privatized and then partially closed during the 1980s, Hawthorne's population declined, underscoring the fact that the community's fate was tied to the expansion and contraction of the federal sphere. Still, over the first century of its existence, the community had learned how to survive on its own in the Nevada desert, and now supporting itself largely by tourism, Hawthorne remains a substantial town.[18]

The survival of its original courthouse was another matter. In the late

1960s, Mineral County commissioners began working on a new facility. By 1974, they had abandoned and condemned the older structure. Surrounded by a chain-link fence for security, the 1885 structure declined and seemed destined for demolition. A grassroots effort in the first decade of the twenty-first century has raised hopes that the building can be saved and used. The fate of no historic building is certain, but it is easy to imagine the Hawthorne courthouse coming back to life as a cultural center.

THOMPSON OPERA HOUSE

Courthouses were one thing, but no nineteenth-century mining town had proven its salt until it could boast having an opera house. Unfortunately, only three Nevada examples survive from the period, namely, those in Virginia City, Eureka, and Pioche. Whereas many communities demolished such monuments to the past, these three mining boomtowns took a different course and invested in their nineteenth-century theaters to pre-

The Thompson Opera House in Pioche is one of three nineteenth-century theaters still standing in Nevada.

serve their remarkable inheritances. Over the years the buildings served in many ways. Traveling actors, itinerant musicians, and local performers displayed their talents in the facilities. The buildings also housed events such as weddings, dances, temperance meetings, and political rallies. The versatile halls were integral to local cultural life for decades.

In 1873, Lincoln County celebrated the opening of its Thompson Opera House in Pioche. The simple wood-frame two-story structure has a front gable facing the street. After serving well for decades, the owners donated the old opera house to Lincoln County in the 1990s. The community then launched a fund-raising drive to finance the building's renovation. Of Nevada's three surviving nineteenth-century opera houses, the one in Pioche is the oldest and the most humble. Like other venues, it played an essential role in its community, serving as everything from a theater and dance hall to a setting for political rallies. As a major restoration nears completion, the building is ready to resume its formal role as a venue for local entertainment. The Thompson Opera House may lack the architectural flamboyance of its counterparts, but it retains the potential to contribute to its community's social life.

The Eureka Opera House followed much the same pattern as its Pioche counterpart, serving for decades as a community center for a remote mining district. This structure benefited from tax revenues generated by Carlin Trend gold mining in the 1980s. It moved to the head of the class when it came to restoration, and so work there was complete by the time the Commission for Cultural Affairs began funding projects in the 1990s.

PIPER'S OPERA HOUSE

John Piper, a German immigrant who arrived in Virginia City in 1860, would become one of the better-known names in the early history of American theater. He began his Comstock career by founding the Old Corner Bar in the commercial center of Virginia City. In 1867, he purchased the prestigious Maguire's Opera House and proved to be an

innovative impresario. Hosting events ranging from bull and bear fights
to Shakespeare, Piper increased the popularity and fame of his venue.

Virginia City's great fire of 1875 devastated the opera house, so Piper
relocated the establishment two blocks uphill, behind his partially damaged Old Corner Bar. In 1883, the opera house burned a second time,
although its original 1863 brick facade survived this fire as well. Undaunted, the persevering entrepreneur, working with the remnants of
the earlier structure, rebuilt his hall and opened it in 1885. An inveter-
ate promoter, Piper made his opera house one of the standard places to
appear when actors, lecturers, or musicians toured the country. He also
endeavored to bring internationally famous performances to Virginia
City. Actors Maud Adams and Edwin Booth, brother of the infamous
assassin John Wilkes Booth, Irish revolutionary Michael Davitt, and John
Philip Souza's band appeared on Piper's stage, and there were many
more.[19] The theater's reputation became so great that performers such as
Houdini and Caruso were said to have appeared there, even though they
did not.[20] For Virginia City residents, it was simply inconceivable that
these great acts would not have performed at Piper's, so they were added,
albeit incorrectly, to the community's opera house lore.

As it stands today, Piper's Opera House is actually a combination of two
structures. The front two-story brick building originally served as Piper's
business block, constructed in 1863. The front facade also includes solid
Romanesque arches and tall doors with large windows that provide ample
light for the interior. When Virginia City was at its height, this building
housed saloons, businesses, and offices. During various phases of its history, it also boasted an apartment and a ticket office.

The opera house is attached to the back of the business block. The
auditorium's floor rests on railroad springs, which gave it a lively bounce
during dances. The proscenium arch, complete with two-story box seat-
ing, embraces the stage. A painting of Shakespeare crowns the arch above
the stage. Canvas covers the ceiling, which is rounded, making the hall
function like a giant megaphone. Its acoustics are beyond compare.

John Piper's Virginia City opera house is one of the more important theaters in the West. The front facade of the building dates to 1863. The auditorium to the rear, the third in a succession of stages, was opened in 1885.

Due to Piper's management, his opera house developed an international reputation that sustained itself even after his death in 1897.[21] At that point, Piper's family continued to run the facility. In 1912, they began showing motion pictures, but the hall still featured live performances from time to time. In 1920, Piper's stage went dark, but the opera house still served as a basketball court and community meeting place. During the 1940s, the hall became a museum. In the 1970s and 1980s, two of Piper's descendants, Louise Zimmer Driggs and her daughter Carol Piper Marshall, sponsored programs and concerts in the facility. They also continued to offer tours of the opera house. By the mid-1990s, the Piper family could no longer maintain the building, so they sold it to a nonprofit organization dedicated to this day to the preservation and continued use of the theater.[22]

Piper's Opera House epitomizes the spirit animating Nevada's first mining boom. Like other people who rushed to Washoe during the early days of the Comstock, John Piper sought his fortune in an unforgiving place. Building on the resources at hand and wedding them to a streak of unsurpassed creativity, he developed a theatrical institution of international renown. When that venue fell—not once, but twice—to flames, Piper displayed a youthful vigor and rebuilt what had been lost. The eternal optimism, strength of character, and dauntless courage required to survive the relentless boom-and-bust cycle of mining communities are inscribed in the very structure of the opera house. And if the structure is "read" properly, the ideals that it embodies will continue to inspire future generations of Nevadans.

THESE FEW BUILDINGS EXEMPLIFY, then, a part of Nevada's early history. Mining was critical to the foundation of the territory and state. The 1860s and 1870s was an explosive, dynamic time when news of Nevada gold and silver inspired excitement throughout the world. Architectural survivors of this period are few, and their scarcity makes them all the more valuable. Using them to view the past, it is possible to acquire a vivid image of a former century. Collectively, the story they tell is one of balancing a desire for permanence with the realization that the mining frontier was transient. Historic buildings from this period are all the more remarkable for the way they fit into this equation. They are testaments to the spirit of a people who survived and even prospered in a harsh and seemingly inhospitable environment.

3 The Other Early Nevada

Nevada's legendary gold and silver deposits sparked rushes and catapulted Nevada to statehood, but mining was not the only industry playing a role in the state's early settlement. Ranchers, railroad workers, craftsmen, merchants, innkeepers, homemakers, and many others also helped develop the region and shape its culture. Their histories are part of the Nevada story, and the buildings they left behind represent attempts to survive in an unforgiving land.

As early as the 1850s, Mormon settlers established farms in the area that would become Nevada, but they were not the first to cultivate crops in the region. Native Americans had engaged in agricultural activities in the Great Basin and in the northern reaches of the Mojave Desert for centuries. Indigenous people cultivated corn, squash, beans, and cotton in the Moapa and Virgin valleys of southern Nevada between roughly fifteen hundred and eight hundred years ago.[1]

Commerce has also long been important to those inhabiting the Great Basin and the Upper Mojave Desert. For centuries, Native Americans used trade routes leading east and west, and as previously noted, Spanish and Mexican traders and explorers traveled along the southern rim of the

Great Basin on their way to California in the eighteenth and nineteenth centuries. British and American fur trappers crisscrossed the lands lying between the Rockies and the Sierra, competing for pelts in the 1820s and 1830s. And as thousands of forty-niners followed wagon trails across Nevada's parched expanses, adventurous entrepreneurs established trading stations across the northern part of the Great Basin along the Humboldt River, along the Truckee River, and in the Carson, Eagle, and Washoe valleys on the eastern slopes of the Sierra Nevada.[2] Situated near water and benefiting from the gold and silver strikes of the 1850s and the 1860s, several of these trading outposts developed into full-fledged communities.

Although these settlements were often less sophisticated than those established by Nevada's miners, some of them survived the decline of boomtowns and the era of *borassca*, as times of mining depression were called, that began around 1880. The secret of survival during these economic hard times, as testified to by these communities, was adaptability and inventiveness. Some survived by catering to the needs of Nevada's farmers and ranchers as regional trading centers, whereas others learned to exploit Nevada's geographical position, lying between California and the East, by catering to the needs of transcontinental travelers, and by developing the rudiments of the state's later highly vaunted tourism industry. In effect, Nevadans were practicing economic diversification as a means of surviving difficult times, long before the term became fashionable in finance and industry.

GOLCONDA SCHOOLHOUSE

One of the settlements that survived the mining depression of the 1880s and 1890s was Golconda. The Golconda Mining District was organized in 1866 during the gold and silver excitement that gripped the state at the time. Two years later, the Central Pacific Railroad, wending its way through Nevada on its transcontinental route, passed through the area and established a stop that took its name from the nearby mining district. Golconda's location, lying along the Humboldt River east of Winnemucca and west of Elko, in northern Nevada's high sagebrush terrain, made it an obvious mercantile center for local mines and ranches. Although area mines repeatedly sprang into existence, the Golconda Mining District was not as profitable as others, and railroading and ranching remained the mainstays of the community. Local hot springs also contributed to the town's economy, giving rise to its reputation as a health spa.[3]

Despite its economic diversity, Golconda remained a modest-sized community. From 1870 to 1900, censuses recorded a population sputtering between eighty and just under five hundred residents. Nevertheless, its economic core was more stable than that of many contemporary towns dependent entirely on mining. In 1888, Golconda could justify con-

The nineteenth-century Golconda Schoolhouse is an impressive architectural statement.

structing a substantial schoolhouse twenty years after the transcontinental railroad had reached the area, and a decade before the town would realize some of its more notable mining successes.

The clapboard-sided one-story Golconda Schoolhouse, designed by J. L. Donnel, represents a vernacular attempt at sophisticated monumental architecture. A striking belfry, clothed in fish-scale shingles and capped with a hipped roof peak, raises the level of the building, allowing it to preside over its setting. Its front entrance opens to a foyer and is capped by a mansard roof with distinct sweeping eaves that provide the structure with a touch of Second Empire Victorian elegance, while supporting the tower above. The bulk of the structure consists of two gabled wings, each housing a distinct classroom. The wings are linked by the front entry space and a cross gable to the rear. In 1929, the school district added a structure at the rear, providing space for a high school. Shed additions on either side of the entrance date to the same period and shelter boys' and girls' restrooms, replacing an earlier privy.

Mineral discoveries after the turn of the century increased Golconda's prosperity and the town grew slightly, but its improved fortunes were short-lived and the community receded to its core population. Nevertheless, the town survived, and its school remained as a monumental expression of its earlier ambitions. Classes at the schoolhouse finally closed in 1966, and the Golconda Fire Protection District assumed management of the facility. Subsequently, the building served as a community center. With the new century, local residents began restoring their revered old schoolhouse. Local mining over the decades has provided intermittent employment, but regardless of changes in the economy, Golconda will certainly persevere and its schoolhouse will remain an integral part of the community.

RAYCRAFT DANCE HALL

Another community that survived the 1880s was Genoa. As noted in chapter 1, Genoa was born during the Utah territorial period, and it went on to

Genoa's Raycraft Dance Hall dates to 1886. The simple wooden structure remains an important community center for Nevada's oldest town.

play an important role in Nevada's western region after statehood. Serving in the last decades of the nineteenth century as Douglas County's first political seat and as a commercial center for the farms and ranches dotting the eastern slopes of the Sierra, by the dawn of the twentieth century the town boasted a fine collection of Victorian-era buildings. Although many of its structures were destroyed during a devastating 1910 town fire, the Raycraft Dance Hall survived along with the town's distinguished courthouse and an intriguing assemblage of other historic buildings.

The dance hall was constructed in 1886, and since 1919, it has been the site of an annual celebration and fund-raiser known as the Candy Dance. While the long wooden structure has an unornamented exterior, its interior features an unusual barrel-vaulted ceiling and attractive wainscot-lined sidewalls. Providing the people of the region with a commodious hall capable of housing a wide variety of events and social functions, the

Raycraft Dance Hall has been a favorite local gathering place for decades. In 1941, the town of Genoa purchased the facility, and it has served as a town hall ever since. In 1977, the town added a porch, and in 1984, the bar from Carson City's Old Globe Saloon was relocated to the hall.

The Genoa town hall, like its courthouse, symbolizes a rural community's endeavor to provide its residents with an element of civilization. Lying far from any metropolitan center, it also reveals the desire for sociability felt by many of Nevada's scattered ranching families. Sturdy but humble and having endured fire and a changing economic climate, the town hall reflects the endurance of the society it serves and the community's aspirations for civility. Even today, as Genoa changes from an agricultural village into a regional resort with Wally's Hot Springs, two golf courses, and hiking in the Sierra, an aura of rural civility characterizes the community.

TRUCKEE MEADOWS RANCHES

Few views of the Nevada landscape were more welcome to westward traveling emigrants than the luxuriant grasses and well-watered expanses of the Truckee Meadows. Referred to by some as "Mist Valley," the lands bounded by the Carson Range to the west and the Virginia Range to the east provided a haven for overland travelers on their way to California. The agricultural possibilities along the course of the river and the commercial opportunities presented by the Emigrant Trail were recognized early in the region's history. By 1852, there were farms and a trading station along the Truckee River. Other ranches and stations supported by overland travelers, local trade with the Comstock, and regional commerce with northern California followed, and several small communities sprang up in the meadows. By the time the transcontinental railroad cut through the area in 1868, the Truckee Meadows was already known for its gardens, ranches, and inns.[4]

A collection of ranch-related buildings dating from 1860 to 1910 recalls the early settlement of the Truckee Meadows and is emblematic of Nevada's alternative nonmining story. In 1868, John S. Bowker established a ranch in the southern part of the Truckee Meadows. He built a barn, bunkhouse, and blacksmith shop, and then sold the complex in 1870 to Peter and Margaret Dalton. The new transcontinental railroad contributed to a growing population and economy throughout northern Nevada and especially along the Truckee River. Rising with this tide, the Daltons expanded the operation from 160 acres to 465 acres. By the close of the nineteenth century, historian Thomas Wren could refer to the ranch as "one of the best . . . in this part of the state."[5] In 1902, the Daltons retired, and Robert T. and Lottie Wilkerson took over the ranch until 1912, when they sold it to the Ferretto family.

One of Nevada's earliest families, the Ferrettos came from Italy and settled in Genoa. In the 1860s, Angelo Ferretto mined on the Comstock and then worked as a teamster, hauling wood and other supplies into Virginia City. In the first decades of the twentieth century, Ferretto and his two sons, John and Joseph, began acquiring local ranches, including the Dalton property.[6] Joseph Ferretto and his wife, Rose, established their home on the Dalton Ranch and raised livestock, alfalfa hay, and wheat. For a time, they also ran a dairy and grew apples and potatoes.

The Ferretto Ranch remained in the family for more than ninety years. As the decades passed, several outbuildings fell into disuse. During the 1990s, developers moved these structures to Boomtown, a truck stop and casino west of Reno. There, they functioned for several years as an old-fashioned setting for the casino's promotional events. These simple, functional wooden buildings were tools rather than statements of architectural design. Sheltered by unornamented rooflines, they featured horizontal clapboard siding or vertical board-and-batten construction, with openings here and there for doors and windows.

At the dawn of the twenty-first century, the weathered wooden structures came to the attention of Truckee Meadows Remembered, a nonprofit group dedicated to preserving Nevada's ranching culture. The organization worked with Washoe County to obtain the structures for

Ranch buildings once dominated the Truckee Meadows, now home to the growing cities of Reno and Sparks. A few of the relics survive.

removal to the county's Bartley Ranch Park, itself one of the last preserves of open space south of Reno. There, the buildings became part of the park's Western Heritage Interpretive Center. These excellent examples of Nevada's nineteenth-century vernacular architecture represent an important chapter in the state's economic history.

GLENDALE SCHOOL

Though less prosperous than Nevada's mining towns, the state's other communities were interested in establishing the impression, if not the reality, of civilization. Like the Raycraft Dance Hall and the Gol-

The Glendale School is a territorial-era structure built in 1863. After decades of service as a center of education, it is now an interpretive center.

conda School, the one-room Glendale School, originally located at Stone and Gates Crossing, serves as an expression of this desire for civility. An agricultural community, the crossing was located in the vicinity of present-day Sparks in the eastern part of the Truckee Meadows. Residents constructed the Glendale schoolhouse at the urging of Erastus C. Sessions, a rancher from Vermont who settled in the Truckee Meadows in 1863. Sessions had opened a school in his home for local children, but there was not enough room. The Glendale School, a white wood-frame building with a large single room, was the solution to this problem.[7]

The humble structure, constructed by Archie Bryant, was barely more than a small box. Eave returns on the gabled ends of the roof recalled Greek Revival architecture. Twin doors on the main facade added to the symmetry of the building. Pairs of windows on the sides could be shuttered closed. An open-air cupola featured wood filigree. Eventually, an unornamented gable-roof addition augmented the front of the building, this time with a single entrance. In addition, workers enclosed the cupola with louvers. Stylistically, this vernacular one-room schoolhouse recalls an architectural type that was characteristic of New England schoolhouses in the nineteenth century. Since Sessions emigrated from Vermont, it is possible that New England inspired the form the Glendale School assumed.[8]

The Glendale School served the Sparks area for nearly a century, becoming a cherished part of the community. Senator Pat McCarran (1876–1954), one of the institution's better-known pupils, once noted that he "had a deep love for the 'little white schoolhouse at the bend in the road.'"[9] In 1958, the Sparks community was finally forced to close the building. In 1976, local residents responded to the threat of vandalism by relocating the school to the grounds of the Reno-Sparks Convention and Visitors Authority on the corner of Virginia Street and Keitzke Lane.

By 1993, it was clear that the school, one of the oldest in the state, suffered from neglect at its new home, so the City of Sparks moved the building to its Victorian Square. An assorted group of dedicated volunteers, including the late Tony Armstrong, before becoming the mayor of Sparks, provided labor for the restoration project. Many people and local groups donated books, report cards, and in some instances even desks belonging to the old school. Eleven months later, the structure was completely restored and equipped with displays detailing the school's history. On October 27, 1994, it opened to the public.[10]

LAKE MANSION

Although Reno's Lake Mansion was constructed less than a generation after the Glendale School, in a cultural sense this handsome Italianate structure seems decades removed from the humble frontier schoolhouse. This home, often called Reno's first residence, represents a grand level of architectural style. As such, it has been an icon of refinement and civility for the entire region for more than a century. W. J. Marsh constructed what would be known as the Lake Mansion on a small rise overlooking the Truckee River in 1877. He used ornate Italianate-style details to decorate the two-story structure. With a hipped roof and widow's walk, and elaborate brackets and window surrounds, his house was one of the Truckee Meadows' more formal expressions of period design. An excellent representation of this occurs in the front doors, which have windows with etched likenesses of the Roman goddess Flora. In addition, the transom above boasts the etched image of a basket full of fruit.

In 1879, Myron Lake purchased the house. Lake, a prominent local developer, owned a toll bridge over the Truckee River, located at the current site of the Virginia Street Bridge. The community that developed around his bridge was first known as Lake's Crossing, but by 1868, the town's name had changed to Reno. For nearly a hundred years, Lake's house stood on the corner of California and Virginia streets, uphill from the original site of the toll bridge. As Reno grew, Lake's house was increasingly threatened by commercial development. In 1971, community leaders acted to prevent the house's demolition by moving it south to the grounds of the Reno-Sparks Convention and Visitors Authority.

Between 1972 and 1982, the Lake Mansion was stabilized, restored, and partially furnished. Washoe Landmark Preservation, Inc., opened the building to the public as a house museum, and the Reno-Sparks Convention and Visitors Authority occasionally used its second floor for office space. In 1995, Washoe Landmark Preservation allowed the nonprofit agency vsa arts of Nevada to use the facility, initiating another phase of renovation of the Lake Mansion. In the late 1990s, the City of

Reno's Lake Mansion has moved twice and now rests near its original 1877 location. It is home to vsa arts of Nevada, a statewide organization.

Reno launched an innovative arts and cultural downtown-redevelopment effort. As the Lake Mansion project progressed, it became clear that the historic house could play a role in the endeavor. In July 2004, the Lake Mansion made the long trek to the corner of Arlington and Court streets, a site near its place of origin. This restless structure with a remarkable past holds great promise for a future serving a growing arts district in Reno.[11]

Functioning today as an art gallery, a community program space, and the permanent home of vsa arts of Nevada, the Lake Mansion adds historic elegance to Reno's downtown. At the same time, it continues to remind contemporary Nevadans of the speed with which the frontier "passed" in the region. In less than a quarter of a century, the rude material culture of Nevada's first settlements was overtaken by sophisticated, high-style forms of architecture.

The Truckee Meadows' rugged ranching culture did not vanish, however, with the arrival of nineteenth-century civilization. Rather, a juxtaposition of these two cultures survived for decades in the meadows, and this coincidence introduced an element of incongruity, if not whimsy, into the valley's cultural life. People who lived along the Truckee River were both pioneers and urbane sophisticates, cowboys and business entrepreneurs, rural and cosmopolitan. A later generation of Nevadans would attempt to capture and indeed exploit the paradoxes animating Reno's culture by labeling it "the biggest little city in the world."

SHERMAN STATION

The desire to infuse a semblance of nineteenth-century civilization into the Nevada wilderness also characterizes Sherman Station in Elko County. Shortly after the turn of the century, Valentine Walther, Nick Scott, and a transient carpenter whose name is now forgotten constructed a two-story bristlecone- and limber-pine log structure on Walther's remote ranch in Huntington Valley. Walther, a native of Germany, was one of the region's first settlers. He had been living in Huntington Valley for more than a quarter of a century before he built his massive log ranch and stage house along Sherman Creek.[12]

Although the logs used in construction are rough-hewn and convey a primitive, rustic origin, this is hardly a frontier log cabin. The large two-story structure includes a handsome bay window and a substantial facade with dormer windows interrupting the roofline. Both bay and dormer windows were often associated in the nineteenth century with the popular Queen Anne and Stick architectural styles. By including these elements in his structure, Walter was, no doubt, attempting to add a bit of grace and refinement to his log home. A sturdy porch with knee brackets and plain cross-board railing also lends this house the feeling that it was built for simple comfort. The material may hark back to frontier roots, belying its rural location, but the overall appearance of the building is reminiscent of a high-style designed building.

Exploiting his ranch's location between Elko, Tuscarora, and Eureka, Walther founded a freight line in the valley in the last decades of the nineteenth century. In 1903, he established a post office and a stage stop on his ranch, which he called Sherman Station. As the nearby mines declined, Tuscarora failed and Walther's freight line became less profitable. Ultimately, he abandoned it and closed the post office. The Walther family remained in Huntington Valley until 1922. After they left, other families moved into Sherman Station and ran the Walther Ranch. At one point, Waddie Mitchell, one of North America's better-known cowboy poets, lived there as a child. Eventually, Sherman Station declined, even serving as a barn.[13]

The old building received a new lease on life in 1997 when the Elko Chamber of Commerce and the City of Elko moved it and several of its outbuildings from Huntington Valley to Elko's City Park to serve as the

Elko County's Sherman Station dates to 1903. The Elko Chamber of Commerce moved the rural stage stop to a city park in 1997.

chamber's headquarters and visitors center.[14] Like the Ferretto Ranch outbuildings, the Glendale Schoolhouse, and the Lake Mansion, Sherman Station was located in a place where preservation was impractical. By moving it into Elko, local history enthusiasts salvaged the structure and preserved the memory of nineteenth-century Nevada's rural culture and Valentine Walther's longing for comfort and civility in the wilds of Huntington Valley.

MESQUITE ROCK HOUSE

Another symbol of the state's agricultural past is the Mesquite Rock House. Like many other communities in southeastern Nevada, Mesquite was founded in the last decades of the nineteenth century by Mormon pioneers. One of its first structures was a simple building now popularly known as the Rock House. It is a remnant of a time when leaders of the Church of Jesus Christ of Latter-day Saints sought to convert the desert lands lying along the Colorado, Virgin, and Muddy rivers to the cultivation of cotton and other warm-weather crops.

In the 1860s, the Mormon leadership called upon its followers to set up colonies in Utah's and Nevada's hot southern regions. The agricultural development of "Utah's Dixie" began with the establishment of farming communities in the upper regions of the Virgin River valley. In 1864, Brigham Young decided to extend the "cotton mission" to include the Muddy River country, and by the close of 1865, the colonies of St. Thomas and St. Joseph perched along the banks of the Muddy River.[15] Although these settlements flourished for a few years, an 1870 boundary survey revealed that they were located in Nevada and not in Utah. Lincoln County officials subsequently decided to collect back taxes, inspiring almost all of the Muddy River colonists to abandon the region. The Mormons renewed their efforts to settle southeastern Nevada in 1877 when another group of Saints settled in the region. This effort ultimately gave rise to two new communities—Bunkerville and Mesquite—in the southern reaches of the Virgin River.

The Mesquite Rock House dates to the 1880s. Silvia E. Potter, a longtime resident, stands in front of her former home.

Situated on the banks of the Virgin River on the Old Spanish Trail, Mesquite's rich soil first attracted the attention of Mormon settlers on their way to the Muddy River colonies. Settlement started fitfully in the 1870s and 1880s, and it included a phase of Mormon communal living. Natural disasters, an unforgiving environment, and internal dissent, sometimes sparked by religious schism, caused the Virgin River settlements to ebb and flow. Periods of collapse were followed by times of expansion as new waves of Mormons entered the region. Eventually, the small farming communities of Bunkerville and Mesquite proved themselves to be successful, and by the dawn of the twentieth century, they were on the path to prosperity.[16]

Dating to the 1880s, the Rock House served several of southern Nevada's historic Mormon families. For example, the first of Dudley

Leavitt's five wives, Mary, lived in the home during the region's second wave of settlement.[17] In the first years of the colonization effort, federal marshals in search of polygamists occasionally caused excitement in the two settlements. Since the founders of these communities were fervent conservative Mormons, some followed the church's early teachings in this regard. After the church condemned plural marriage in 1890, however, most of those engaging in polygamy abandoned it, and law enforcement officials ultimately ceased their raids into these communities.

The Rock House is a humble one-story vernacular building. The house's steeply pitched roof is exaggerated as it connects with the sloping roof of a large porch. It has thick rock walls covered in plaster. In the early twentieth century, owners replaced the roof and completed two adobe brick additions. Bath- and laundry rooms were welcome additions in the 1970s. The replacement of wooden floors with concrete eliminated some of the historic fabric, but the building, together with the surrounding gardens and trees, is preserved as a testament to its past. People lived in the house until 2003.[18]

For decades, Mesquite and Bunkerville survived as modest agricultural communities. In the 1980s, they began expanding rapidly, benefiting from an influx of retirees as well as from their geographic position, lying midway between the Mormon cities of southern Utah and Nevada's bur-geoning tourist mecca, Las Vegas. During the 1990s, in fact, Mesquite was the fastest-growing community in Nevada, and it boasted its own thriving tourist industry.[19]

Population expansion and economic growth often threaten the historic remnants of a community's past. To protect a vestige of its heritage, the City of Mesquite purchased the historic Rock House at the dawn of the twenty-first century. When the city acquired the building, local residents were hoping to preserve it for public use. Although the community has considered various options to salvage the Rock House, it remains in jeop-ardy. The unassuming structure requires considerable restoration, and its potential to serve the community is limited. Nevertheless, the historic structure represents an early attempt to confront a harsh environment and make it home by utilizing materials at hand in a sparse terrain.

J. A. WADSWORTH GENERAL STORE

The J. A. Wadsworth General Store, located in Panaca, also highlights the perseverance of Nevada's early adherents of the Church of Jesus Christ of Latter-day Saints. Like Mesquite, Panaca was founded by Mormon pioneers in the mid-1860s. In the wake of mining strikes in the Meadow and Pahranagat valleys, Nevada's congressional delegation drafted a bill ceding a portion of Utah's western lands to Nevada. Since the Mormon-dominated Utah Territory was still at loggerheads with the federal government over polygamy and the desire among the religion's leaders to create a sovereign nation, the bill passed and Panaca along with the local mines became part of Nevada.[20]

Situated on an eastern spur of the Ely Mountains, Pioche became the seat of Lincoln County and the center of the region's mining industry. Panaca, on the other hand, was established below, in a valley where agriculture could thrive. Although the two communities were only twelve miles apart, the cultural gap between them could not have been greater. During its early years, Pioche was famed as a raucous, violent mining camp, whereas Panaca's sober and pious Latter-day Saints developed a sedate agricultural community. Nonetheless, the two towns depended on one another, since the miners required agricultural produce and the Mormon community needed a market for its crops.[21] Commerce was crucial, then, to Panaca's survival, and this historical reality is testified to by the J. A. Wadsworth General Store.

The two-story adobe-brick building dates to the 1880s. Adobe, as noted in chapter 1, was a favorite building material of the Mormons. Adobe's constituent elements, clay and sand, were readily available in the Intermountain West, and it was well suited to the extremes of heat and cold plaguing the region. Durable and practical, adobe reflects the sturdy spirit of the region's early settlers. The general store also provides schol-

The J. A. Wadsworth General Store in Panaca served the Lincoln County agricultural community beginning in the 1880s.

ars with evidence of the Mormons' communal spirit, since their fraternal ethos is important to the store's early history. It functioned for many years as Panaca's commercial center, but it also served as a community meeting place, and for a time the local school district used it.

During the 1990s, the Panaca Heritage Center Committee began restoring the durable old structure to convert it into a museum and visitors center. They replaced the store's roof and added a porch. Recalling the early Mormon community spirit, the restoration of the general store received solid local support. The adaptable structure soon became a valued resource, honoring a distinguished heritage and providing insight into the culture of Nevada's early Mormon settlers.[22]

LOVELOCK DEPOT

The wheels of trade were essential to the survival of Nevada's far-flung agricultural communities, and during the nineteenth century, those wheels often turned on iron rails. Lovelock's Central Pacific Railroad depot serves as an excellent example of the transportation industry's contribution to Nevada history. Located about ninety miles northeast of Reno in the lower Humboldt River valley, Lovelock occupies a site that was once called Big Meadows. This inviting expanse of grassland was the last place where westward-bound emigrants could take on water before venturing into the most perilous portion of their journey, the trek across the notorious Forty-Mile Desert. As such, several trading posts were founded in the area during the 1840s, but permanent Euro-American settlements were not established there until the 1860s.[23]

George Lovelock, an ambitious Englishman, was one of the area's first settlers. When the Central Pacific Railroad laid track through Big Meadows in the summer of 1868, Lovelock donated eighty-five acres of land to serve as a railroad-town site. In exchange, Charles Crocker, the Central Pacific's construction manager, called the site "Lovelock's Station." By 1879, Lovelock's Station had grown to include sixty souls, and the Central Pacific decided to construct a state-of-the-art facility for the community. Completed in 1880, the Eastlake-style depot was designated a "class A" station, which meant that it could receive "all type of freight and in large quantities."[24]

The building is a remarkable expression of high-style design. Knee brackets supporting exaggerated eaves to protect customers waiting for a train give the structure a classic depot appearance. Exaggerated trim boards, painted in contrasting colors to accentuate the lines, define the Eastlake style. Capping the gables are ornate spires, testimony to the Central Pacific's commitment to building with style rather than cheaper simplicity. The depot's refined architecture also hints at the railroad's power and wealth in America's "Gilded Age."

Lovelock's railroad depot, completed in 1880, is an excellent expression of Eastlake-style design.

The Southern Pacific acquired the Central Pacific at the turn of the century, but it continued to use the depot until the 1990s, when the railroad finally closed the facility. The Southern Pacific considered demolishing the old depot, but in 1996, it decided to donate the building to the City of Lovelock. The corporation also generously included the funds designated for demolition as part of the donation. The city used this support to relocate the depot and place it on a secure foundation. In 2001, Lovelock began renovating the depot, which now functions as an exhibition center and sandwich shop.

BREWERY ARTS CENTER

Carson City was another Nevada community that survived the collapse of Nevada's mines during the last decades of the nineteenth century. The town, nestled on the eastern slopes of the Sierra Nevada in Eagle Valley, served as a center of government, but it also catered to the agricultural needs of local ranchers. In addition, it was home to a U.S. Mint and to the Virginia and Truckee Railroad Shops, adding to the community's economic viability. West of the fabulous mines of Virginia City, north of the prosperous farms of the Carson Valley, and south of Reno and the transcontinental railroad, Carson City functioned early on as a regional trading center.

The area's potential as a commercial center was, no doubt, uppermost in the minds of Abraham Curry and his partners when they purchased Eagle Ranch, the future site of Carson City, in 1858. Little besides Curry's audaciousness, however, explains his inclusion of a ten-acre central plaza for the erection of a state capitol in his town plan, a design he implemented three years before Carson City became the capital of the newly created Nevada Territory.[25] Needless to say, the town's position as state capital contributed to its viability. The economic engine of government was a reliable source of income, allowing the community to endure the periodic doldrums of the late nineteenth century.

Two neighboring Carson City structures, the Carson Brewery Building and Saint Teresa of Avila Catholic Church, mirror the community's history and serve as examples of Nevada's diverse life during the nineteenth century. Although they were originally far apart in purpose, they now operate under a common umbrella.

When Jacob Klein and John Wagner founded the Carson Brewery on Second Street between Minnesota and Division streets in 1860, Nevada did not yet exist. Carson City was little more than a cluster of buildings erected on the former Eagle Ranch. Over the ensuing years, the fate of Klein and Wagner's brewery paralleled Carson City's good fortune. By 1864, when Nevada attained statehood, the owners had expanded into a newly built two-story facility on the corner of West King and South Division streets. The first floor housed the brewery and a bar that remained popular with Carson City residents for generations. The building also served the community as an ice plant, while its second-floor hall provided space for Nevada's first lodge of the Free and Accepted Masons.[26]

Klein and Wagner's brewery building dates to an early period of Nevada history, but it is nevertheless a stout expression of permanence. Its elegant second-floor meeting hall also recalls the spirit of conviviality and fraternity that characterized Nevada's nineteenth-century frontier communities. Large windows open on the main floor for a view of King Street. The second floor exhibits tall windows with segmented curved

The old brewery in Carson City dates to 1864. The structure served fraternal organizations and the local newspaper before becoming home to an arts center.

arches, allowing natural light to illuminate the meeting room, which could remain private because of its elevation. The hall's beautiful pressed-tin ceiling with details accented with original paint remains as an expression of the opulence of the structure. Along the roofline, the ornate use of brick forms an attractive row of dentils to define the cornice.

In 1879, Wagner sold his interest in the brewery to Klein, who operated the business until his death in 1899. James Raycraft and Frank Golden then ran the business as the Carson Brewing Company for a decade. Max Stenz, a Bavarian immigrant, next acquired the brewery, and in 1913, he converted from steam to lager beer. Stenz promoted his Tahoe Beer, with the slogan "Famous as the Lake."[27]

Under Stenz's management, the brewery flourished until the advent of Prohibition in 1920. Undaunted, Stenz successfully converted the facility to the production of legal "near beer." In 1926, he turned the business over to his son-in-law, Arnold Millard. During the Depression, sales declined, but the collapse of Prohibition in 1933 increased profits. While running the brewery, Millard served two terms as Carson City's mayor. As World War II raged, the brewery continued to operate, but when large corporate producers took control of America's brewing industry after the war, sales declined, forcing Millard to liquidate the business in 1948.

For a time, the building's fate was uncertain. In 1950, Donald W. Reynolds purchased the former brewery and used it as the production plant for the *Nevada Appeal*, Nevada's oldest surviving daily newspaper. In 1974, the *Appeal* moved its operations to Bath Street, and the aged building's fate was once again left to chance. Fortune, however, was kind to the old brewery. In 1975, Carson City commemorated the centennial of its incorporation, and the following year the United States celebrated its bicentennial. In honor of these two anniversaries, Carson City formed a Centennial-Bicentennial Commission, which turned to the old brewery as one of its projects. Over the next several years, the Brewery Arts Center, formerly the Carson City Arts Alliance, began working to purchase and transform the building into a multipurpose community arts center. The property soon housed a classroom, workshop, pottery studio, visual-arts gallery, and theater.

SAINT TERESA OF AVILA CATHOLIC CHURCH

At the dawn of the new millennium, the Brewery Arts Center expanded west to include the Saint Teresa of Avila Catholic Church. The church was founded in 1861, and it serves as yet another reminder that early Nevadans were determined to live civilly despite the harsh frontier. Whereas most were drawn to Nevada for economic reasons, a few came to the state to tend to the spiritual needs of its early ranchers, merchants, and miners. According to several of Nevada's first ministers, this was no easy task. In 1874, an agent of the California Bible Society expressed his views on the state's religiosity in the following words: "Is there a State in our whole Union where there is so little religious restraint, such ignorance of the Bible, such flaunting at its teachings, such Sabbath-breaking, such heaven-daring profanity, such common drunkenness, such unblushing licentiousness, and such glorying in shame—in short, is there another State where people so generally feel as though they were almost or quite out of God's moral jurisdiction?"[28]

During the early days of settlement, religious buildings in Nevada were hard to come by, and those citizens intending to attend services had to make do with what was available. The history of Carson City's Catholic church is emblematic of this problem. Father Hugh Gallagher erected the town's first house of Catholic worship in the early 1860s. This building blew down. The parish rebuilt it once or twice more (the record is unclear) only to see its church succumb again to Eagle Valley's fierce winds.[29]

In 1865, Father John Curley finally constructed an edifice that survived Eagle Valley's gusts. Nevertheless, five years later Father John Grace demolished Curley's church and erected a new structure in its place. His church, dedicated to Saint Teresa of Avila, remains standing to this day, although it has changed in profound ways. The original church was a wood-frame structure with a tall tower and steeple. Pointed arches for the windows lent traditional ecclesiastical elements to the design.

Carson City's Saint Teresa of Avila Catholic Church saw many alterations since its construction in 1870. Today, it serves as a theater for the Brewery Arts Center.

Saint Teresa's eventually began to show its age, and, unfortunately, a series of additions and modifications obscured the Gothic Revival building. In the 1930s, Father Henry Wientjes redecorated the church with murals, and in 1949, he added a brick veneer that hid the original wooden fabric. The 1949 project also replaced the foundation with a concrete substructure that included basement rooms.[30] In spite of these alterations, the interior of the main church hall retained its historic feel.

In 1980, Father Lawrence Quilici responded to decades of growth by working on an expansion of the church. In spite of this, the congregation had completely outgrown the space by the late 1990s. At that time, the congregation decided to move to a larger facility.

Saint Teresa's acoustics impressed Brewery Arts officials, who recognized its potential as a fine performing-arts facility. They subsequently negotiated with the ecclesiastical hierarchy for the building's purchase, which they achieved at the beginning of the new century. Workers moved many of the original leaded-glass windows to the new church, providing it with a link to the institution's past and relieving the Brewery Arts Center of the need to address a resource not in keeping with its mission. The historic church building now serves as a performance hall, benefiting the entire community in this new capacity.

AS A WHOLE, Nevada's nineteenth-century buildings reflect an attempt to settle the western wilds, employing sophisticated forms of architecture as soon it was possible. Mining towns followed a familiar pattern, prospering and failing with the location and exhaustion of ore bodies. Their history and architecture, like the economy they commanded, dominated the young territory and state, but there was another side to Nevada. Many communities developed in response to agricultural and commercial opportunities, and these places also possessed an architectural heritage. Unlike the mining towns, communities grounded in agriculture and commerce tended to survive periods of depression without withering and blowing away. Their buildings typically found more consistent use than their mining-town counterparts. This situation posed both a challenge and a benefit for those promoting the preservation of Nevada's past. Use can cause change and demolition, and economic depression often results in short-term preservation through neglect and abandonment. Whatever path followed by these vestiges of the past, their survival was predicated upon their ability to meet the needs of Nevada's ever-changing culture and society.

4 A New Century

At the turn of the twentieth century, a new mining boom energized the state. Discoveries in central Nevada generated dozens of rich gold, silver, and copper mines, and two desert metropolises, Tonopah and Goldfield, emerged. In a parallel development, copper mines in eastern Nevada flourished to the benefit of communities there. In many ways, this period of wealth and excitement mirrored the 1860s. People rushed to Nevada's "wastelands" to exploit mining opportunities, and once in the region, they contrived new ways to deal with its harsh environment. Many prospered. Still, as in Nevada's first great mining boom, most became wageworkers. Although numerous parallels exist between the state's first great mining boom and its second, Nevada's early-twentieth-century economy was more complex than that of the nineteenth century, and this affected its social and cultural development. Turn-of-the-century buildings reflected the opulence of the new bonanzas, but they also testified to an increasing reliance on agriculture and the transportation industry.[1]

RICHARDSON HOUSE

As the transcontinental railroad continued north and east from Reno, it passed through Lovelock and proceeded to Winnemucca, a town with roots reaching back to 1850. At that time, the settlement, originally called French Ford, French Bridge, or Centerville, was known for its bridge across the Humboldt River. In 1866, a post office at the site took the formal name of Winnemucca, paying homage to a leading family among the region's Northern Paiutes.[2]

Humboldt County, organized in 1861, included a large part of north-central Nevada. Its county seat was the thriving mining town of Unionville. When its mines failed, community leaders in Winnemucca agitated for a move of government, finally succeeding in this endeavor in 1873. Benefiting from its geographical location, the town developed as a commercial hub, a railroad stop, and a center of government. With a long-lasting, stable economic foundation, a sizable stock of substantial buildings emerged in the community, and many of these historic structures survive to this day.[3]

Among Winnemucca's historic resources is a house that is easily overlooked. In 1899, W. A. Cumley decided to build a home in Winnemucca. Although turn-of-the-century Nevada was on the verge of a mineral rush that would soon rival any other in the history of the United States, it was not possible to foresee that event. By erecting his house when he did, Cumley unknowingly anticipated the statewide development that was right around the corner. The building is not remarkable in most respects, but it is a good example of the type of places where local workers lived and raised families.

The house is an excellent, humble expression of Eastlake—style architecture. More important, it also recalls the significance of Cornish immigrants to the development of the state. Cumley sold it in 1902 to Albert E. and Annie Pearce Richardson. Albert's and Annie's parents had come from Cornwall, the southwestern extremity of Britain, known for millennia for its mining. Because the family was Cornish, fellow immigrants arriving in Winnemucca were known to stay there. After it was in the family for 102 years, a descendant, Nora Saunders Chipman, donated the house to the North Central Nevada Historical Society. The society subse-

Winnemucca's Richardson House was built in 1899. The house is tied to the story of immigration from Cornwall, a British center of mining.

quently moved the building to its property, where it stands today, allowing visitors a view of local history, mining, and immigration.

Cornish miners were naturally attracted to the American West. They were experts at hard-rock mining, so they shunned the eastern coalfields as well as the placer mining of the California gold country. Instead, they watched for mines that went underground and then frequently arrived to take the best jobs, including those in management. Tiny Cornwall probably contributed no more than one hundred thousand immigrants to the international mining frontier during the nineteenth century. Well over one thousand of these immigrants settled in Nevada at one time or another, having a tremendous effect on the development of the state's industry. These "Cousin Jacks," as they were often called, typically arrived as single men and left quickly when ore bodies became exhausted and opportunities presented themselves elsewhere. Occasionally, Cornish women came with the men, and when that occurred, there was a greater chance that the immigrants would linger after mines failed. This was certainly the case with the Richardson and Pearce families, who have descendants throughout northern Nevada.[4]

The modest Richardson House exhibits well-executed design and details. It features spindles along a porch frieze, a jigsawn decorative gable cornice, and curved brackets. The projecting wing with clipped faces for side windows and the shingle patterns in the gable ends are also typical of the style. The two cornice gables and particularly well-crafted decorations give the house a distinctive look. The Eastlake style's concern with simplicity and functional design perhaps appealed to the practicality of Nevada's Cornish-immigrant families.

TONOPAH MINING PARK

Construction of the Richardson House occurred only one year before a pivotal event in the history of world mining. On May 19, 1900, Jim Butler, an erstwhile miner-turned-rancher, discovered silver in Nye County's San Antonio Range. Butler asked future governor Tasker L. Oddie, who at that time was a young lawyer living in Austin, Nevada, to have the samples assayed. The tests revealed the ore was worth more than three hundred dollars a ton. News of Butler's strike and its extraordinarily rich ore spread rapidly, and Nevada experienced another great mining rush. Tonopah, a new boomtown, emerged as a center of activity, and Nevada's economy, in the doldrums since the 1880s, underwent a renaissance.[5] A surveyor from Austin quickly platted the new town, and miners' tents soon gave way to permanent structures erected from materials freighted in from Reno, more than two hundred miles to Tonopah's northwest. Within months, head frames, mills, and other industrial buildings littered the landscape. At the same time, the town experienced a flurry of commerce, and a substantial business district emerged. When Tonopah inherited the seat of Nye County from the dwindling nineteenth-century mining town of Belmont in 1905, the profits of government were added to the town's rapidly expanding economic base.

During the early twentieth century, Tonopah was one of Nevada's most prosperous communities, but during the 1920s, the inevitable decline in mining began. The community survived the Great Depression of the 1930s primarily because it was a county seat. After World War II, occasional increases in the price of gold and silver jolted local mining back to life, but the hope this offered was too often short-lived. In the 1980s, molybdenum and copper mining reenergized the town. The production of these

Tonopah boasts one of the nation's finest parks devoted to mining history. The site includes hoisting works and excavations of several of the town's more important early-twentieth-century mines.

ores was as vulnerable, however, to the boom-and-bust cycle as the production of gold and silver had been, and so the good times of the 1980s also faded.[6]

More important to the community's longevity was its proximity to federal lands and the expansion of the nation's atomic energy and defense industries during the mid-twentieth century. Taking advantage of Nevada's vast and open terrain, the Army Air Corps trained pilots during World War II at the Tonopah Army Air Base, about seven miles east of town. In addition, in the 1950s, the Tonopah Test Range, roughly thirty miles south of Tonopah, began serving a variety of uses associated with weapons testing on behalf of the Department of Energy.[7]

Although Tonopah benefited from the dramatic expansion of the nation's defense industry during the last half of the twentieth century, it also profited from the development of the federal highway system and the growth of the state's tourism industry. Lying roughly midway between Las Vegas and Reno and situated at the junction of U.S. Route 6 on the Grand Army of the Republic Highway and U.S. Route 95, the community has long served as an overnight resting stop for weary travelers.[8]

During the 1970s, community leaders recognized that it might be possible to capitalize on the tourism trade by promoting the preservation and use of Tonopah's many historic resources. In the early 1980s, for example, investors reopened Tonopah's famed Mizpah Hotel. The business sputtered economically but became a cornerstone of the effort to market Tonopah as a center of cultural tourism.

Another attempt to bolster the town's economy by appealing to cultural tourism was the opening of the Tonopah Mining Park in 1994. Located in the area of Jim Butler's original strike and devoted to preserving central Nevada's mining heritage, Tonopah's open-air museum boasts numerous artifacts and several significant structures dating from the earliest period of mining in the region. Intact and well-preserved head frames, power plants, ore bins, steam shovels, and mine stopes, as well as an ore crusher, a five-stamp mill, a roller mill, and hoist houses, survive on a site where four mining companies once operated. At their peak, these companies sustained a town and caused the entire region to flourish.

The vernacular structures preserved at the park testify to the practicality of mining architecture. Investors constructed utilitarian buildings to extract precious metals efficiently from the ground. Typically, these steel boxes with a few doors and windows were not designed for aesthetics. In addition, permanence was not a goal, but these structures were substantial enough to support the heavy equipment needed for the job at hand. The hoisting work, a timbered-frame structure supporting a large wheel at its top, is an unofficial symbol of Nevada mining, and Tonopah had more than its share. Scattered across the state's landscape, many of these sentinels from the past survive to recall former glories, but they are rarely offered to the public for interpretation. Still, few aspects of Nevada's material culture at the dawn of the twentieth century testify more eloquently to the energy, resourcefulness, and technological sophistication of the state's miners than the industrial architecture they left behind.

NYE COUNTY COURTHOUSE

Tonopah is also home to a wide variety of nonindustrial historic structures that date to its bonanza era. The Nye County Courthouse, the Tonopah fire station, and the building that now serves as the town library are reminders of everyday life in a burgeoning and prosperous early-twentieth-century Nevada community.

The Nye County Courthouse survives as an early attempt at high-style architectural design. Within months of the 1905 transfer of the county seat from Belmont to Tonopah, Nye County began constructing a new courthouse. The architect, J. C. Robertson, designed the structure with elements of the then popular Romanesque Revival style. Details included rough-hewn coursed ashlar stone and a rounded arch supported by clustered columns for the front entrance. A peculiar bullet-shaped dome

The Tonopah Volunteer Fire Department built its facility in 1907. Fire damaged the structure in 1920, but the community made repairs and continued to use the old firehouse.

FACING PAGE:

FACING PAGE:

TOP: Nye County began constructing its Tonopah courthouse in 1905, but it built several additions throughout the twentieth century.

BOTTOM: Tonopah's 1906 library was not replaced until 2001.

crowns the building. In 1907, Robertson provided plans for a two-story jail addition, and in 1960, the county erected further additions to the courthouse.[9]

Few high-style forms of architecture were better suited to the rough culture of a mining town than Romanesque Revival. As architectural historian James D. Van Trump notes, this robust style displayed an "earthiness" and a "pragmatism" that appealed to the taste of industrial America. At the same time, Romanesque Revival's emphasis on a structure's mass and volume, as well as its frequent use of rough brick or quarried stone, marked it with a weight and authority appropriate for public buildings. Moreover, the style's rugged but romantic appeal to the mythic Anglo-Saxon roots of the American people dovetailed with the way many of Nevada's turn-of-the-century miners viewed themselves.[10]

The courthouse served Nye County for almost nine decades before it was replaced by another facility in the mid-1990s. For a time, the old building was left in disrepair. Beginning in 2004, however, the county began to address its responsibility as custodian of one of the state's more remarkable public buildings. It initiated a preservation program and sought uses for the structure, a process that continues to unfold.

TONOPAH LIBRARY

Until 2001, Tonopah could boast having the oldest building in Nevada that was continuously used as a public library. At the beginning of the millennium, the town moved its library into a new facility, but the institution's roots reach back to Tonopah's inception at the dawn of the twentieth century. The story began with the 1901 death of John Randal Weeks, allegedly the first person buried in the new town. His passing inspired his brother, a resident of Alameda, California, to donate two hundred books to start a library. Responding to this generous donation, local women raised funds for the library. Construction of the facility was completed in 1906.

John J. Hill served as both architect and builder, producing a simple single-story structure with a hipped roof. Stone for the project came from the base of nearby Mount Brougher. Whereas the building's sidewalls are composed of random rough-cut material, its front presents a more refined image, with dressed coursed stone with a central door balanced on either side by one-over-one tall windows. Half windows on the sides allowed for more bookshelves in its interior. Although the porch was later enclosed, the humble facility remains as one of the best-preserved examples of early stone construction in Tonopah.[11] The historic library offers a reminder of a paradox often encountered in Nevada's mining culture: contradicting what intuition might conclude, rough-and-tumble mining communities valued literacy and education.

TONOPAH VOLUNTEER FIREHOUSE

The Tonopah Volunteer Firehouse, a simple structure for a community service essential to arid boomtowns of the Intermountain West, dates to 1907. In that year, the Nye County Commission appointed a chief to its volunteer fire department, and he subsequently commissioned the construction of a firehouse. An attached gymnasium in the rear was built the following year to provide firefighters with a place to recreate. Ironically, a fire damaged the firehouse in 1920, but the local government funded its restoration, complete with metal siding to inhibit future fires.

In their post-1920 form, the firehouse and gymnasium are simple adjacent structures clad in corrugated metal with false fronts. Plain brackets, crafted in metal, support a simple cornice at the top of the false fronts. The firehouse is composed of two-story and one-story buildings next to one another and the gymnasium to the rear. The gym features a well-preserved hardwood floor. In all, the structures exhibit the sort of pragmatic, vernacular approach to design typical of nineteenth-century and early-twentieth-century mining camps. Lacking a sizable tax base after Tonopah's turn-of-the-century boom period, the community watched as the firehouse complex sank into disrepair. Analysis will determine if the historic resource can be saved and put to new use.

ESMERALDA COUNTY COURTHOUSE

Jim Butler's silver and gold strike at Tonopah spawned a wave of mineral exploration. As in the 1860s, wandering prospectors fanned out across Nevada seeking new discoveries. As before, a series of strikes ensued, giving rise to such well-known mining towns as Rhyolite, Rawhide, and Searchlight as well as to Goldfield, the most famous of them all. Playing a role that was the stuff of legend, Butler was also central to the discovery of Goldfield's mines. In 1902, he grubstaked two young miners, William Marsh and Harry Stimler, who unearthed one of Nevada's richest gold deposits, located about twenty-five miles south of Tonopah.[12] As news of the rich ore spread, thousands flocked to the site, making the stampede to Goldfield the last great rush in the continental United States. For several years, Goldfield was Nevada's largest city. A prosperous center of industry, it was lively and progressive with a penchant for self-promotion. Buoyed by its mineral wealth and confident of its future, Goldfield wrested Esmeralda's county seat from Hawthorne in 1907, and it immediately planned for the construction of one of Nevada's more substantial courthouses.

At the very moment the city began building its courthouse, a symbol of prosperity and aspirations for the future, a labor conflict shook the community. Leaders of the Western Federation of Miners and the Industrial Workers of the World, often called the Wobblies, were organizing aggressively in Goldfield. The mine owners, led by George Wingfield, decided to drive the militant unionists out of town. Using an infamous murder trial involving union members, mine owners exaggerated reports of union violence to persuade Nevada governor John T. Sparks to ask President Theodore Roosevelt to send federal troops to Goldfield. Protected by the United States Army, the mine owners then slashed wages and forced the miners to sign statements that they were not and never had been members of the Miners' Union. The mines then hired scab workers to replace union members. Within a matter of months, the owners had extinguished militant unionism in Goldfield. Although a presidential commission found no justification for calling in federal troops, the union leaders had been

Esmeralda County employs one of the best-preserved turn-of-the-century courtrooms in Nevada.

defeated, and the mine owners asserted their unchallenged hegemony over the community.[13]

The Esmeralda County Courthouse was constructed in the midst of Goldfield's labor strife, and although it is difficult to understand the inspiration for its architecture, the building's commanding presence suggests the triumph of authority over the forces of insurrection. Constructed in 1907 by Salt Lake City's John Shea at the height of Goldfield's labor conflict, the courthouse became an imposing symbol of law and order. Although the two-story rusticated-stone structure possesses Mission Revival features, its battlement-like parapet gives it the look of a medieval fortress. The imposing facade is at once one of the most troubling and distinctive of Nevada public buildings.[14]

The town of Goldfield survived the labor dispute, and it flourished for another decade. At the close of the First World War, the mining town began to decline. Devastated by two fires in the 1920s, little remains today of what was once Nevada's greatest city. Fortunately, the massive courthouse survives. Goldfield still functions as the seat of government for Esmeralda County, and its courthouse has taken on the role of local museum, where people can step through an open door into another century.

GOLDFIELD FIREHOUSE

Another reminder of Goldfield's glory days is the community firehouse. Echoing the choice Tonopah residents made to save their historic firehouse, Goldfield residents also examined the possibilities of restoring

Esmeralda County moved its seat of government from Hawthorne to the newly founded boomtown of Goldfield in 1907. Community leaders quickly built a courthouse *(left)* and a firehouse *(right)*, erecting two substantial buildings in the center of town.

the building that once housed the men who risked their lives to fight the community's great conflagrations. Completed in 1908, the Goldfield Firehouse was a response to public outcries for a more appropriate facility to house the town's fire-protection equipment. This more elaborate building is the two story stone structure that stands next to the modern Highway 95 as it passes through Goldfield. The building boasts a decorative metal cornice with dentils, and it is surmounted by a stone parapet.

The front facade of the 1908 firehouse features a large double doorway with a sign that reads "Fire Station No. 1." Windows above and to the side of the doorway provide light to the first and second floors. Doorways and windows pierce the structure's sidewalls, but to its rear is a large second-story double door for access to the hayloft, reflecting a time when horses pulled the firemen's equipment. Double doors on the main floor allowed teams to exit from the front or back. The attractive building's simple design, though cost-effective, provided substantial accommodations for an essential public service.

As the community declined, so did its ability to support the facility and its full-time firefighting staff. Eventually, the structure was abandoned and left to the elements. The firehouse still stands as a monument to civic consciousness in the early twentieth century. Town leaders have examined what would be needed to save and use the building, but its future remains a matter of question.

SMOKY VALLEY LIBRARY

Manhattan is one of the smaller camps that sprang into existence in the wake of Jim Butler's turn-of-the-century strike. Prospectors established the mining district, located in Nye County to the north of Tonopah, in the 1860s, during the first great period of exploration in the Great Basin. Manhattan dates only to 1905, however, during the state's second era of mining excitement. Within a year of its founding, the town could boast nearly three thousand residents. With local mines enjoying continued production, Manhattan assumed the appearance of stability. Teachers

Manhattan, a mining camp in Nye County, uses its 1906 schoolhouse as a library.

began instructing young scholars there as early as 1906, and in 1912, the community assumed the task of constructing a schoolhouse. It opened at the beginning of the 1913 school year.

Local contractor Angus McDonald built the structure, which drew on the fashions of the day by employing elements of Colonial Revival–style architecture. The lack of a unified design indicates that McDonald was not an architect, and the building must be regarded as vernacular and intuitively planned. The building includes a central entry foyer, hipped roof, and front pedimented gable. Of particular note are its elaborate pressed-tin ceilings and wall coverings. Originally, exterior siding also featured pressed-metal panels to imitate stone, but this was covered by stucco at some point.

Gold production lasted several years in Manhattan, but its ore was limited and the community was destined to fade. Declining production resulted in a depression in the 1920s. Technological innovations and other factors combined to help the struggling town. In 1942 the Roosevelt administration placed wartime restrictions on gold mining, and the community's future seemed bleak, even though Senator Pat McCarran persuaded the administration to allow limited dredge mining in the vicinity. Manhattan's population continued to decline, and for want of a reasonable number of students, the old schoolhouse finally closed in 1955. It remained empty for decades.[15]

During the 1960s and 1970s, Manhattan's population dwindled until it teetered on the edge of becoming a completely abandoned ghost town. The community enjoyed something of a rebirth, however, in the 1980s, when the price of gold began to soar and new technologies allowed miners to retrieve trace amounts of microscopic gold. At that time, the old school reopened as the Smoky Valley Library.

The Manhattan school's outhouse is also of historic note. This humble structure is no ordinary facility, for it is a remnant of the Works Progress Administration's "fly-proof privy" program of the 1930s. Although approximately eleven hundred such structures were built with federal assistance in Nevada, few survive. When the library took over the facility in the 1980s, the privy continued to serve, and as one librarian noted, the institution had Internet access before it acquired indoor plumbing.[16]

JARBIDGE COMMUNITY CENTER

A 1909 gold strike in the Jarbidge Mountains of northern Nevada launched a rush to the region, and almost overnight a town appeared. Located roughly four hundred miles north of Tonopah, near the Nevada-Idaho boundary, the Jarbidge strike was one of the last made in Nevada during its early-twentieth-century boom. Nestled in Elko County's awe-inspiring Jarbidge Range, the town lies in a valley so removed from the rest of the state that once the snow falls, it can be accessed only through Idaho. The town's odd name, often mistakenly referred to as "Jarbridge," is taken from the mountain range in which it resides. Its etymology is confused, drawing on real or imagined Native American terms supposedly meaning "devil."

The town grew rapidly after the 1909 strike, and residents in the isolated community quickly felt a need for a social gathering place. Jar-

The Jarbidge Community Center was built in 1910 and has served the rural Elko County town since that time.

bidge's leading citizens hired a carpenter, H. W. Hiscock, and a miner, John Siittig, to build a much needed facility. They financed the structure by selling charter memberships in the "Jarbidge Community Club," and construction began in August 1910. The building was rushed to completion, opening in time for the town's Thanksgiving celebration.[17]

The open hall was made of logs with chinking to seal the walls. The lack of a ceiling exposed the truss system, contributing to the barnlike feel of the structure. A corrugated-metal roof, complete with siren, caps the hall. The building lacks a formal design, making it an example of vernacular architecture. It is reminiscent of first-settlement structures common to the state during the 1850s and 1860s, but this sort of rustic construction fifty years later testifies to the fact that in the remote Jarbidge Mining District, the frontier—a wild, untamed space where wilderness intersects with civilization—lingered in Nevada into the twentieth century.

Jarbidge flourished as a mining camp for several years. At its height the community boasted fifteen hundred citizens. In 1919, the Jarbidge Mining District produced more gold than anywhere else in the state, but poor production at that time set the bar fairly low in Nevada.[18] By the mid-1930s, the gold mine at Jarbidge had failed, and the community declined. Its citizens dispersed, and by the outbreak of World War II, only eight people lived there.

Those who remained continued to use their historic hall as a meeting space and museum. The building hosted barbecues and dances and annual celebrations for May Day, Memorial Day, and the Fourth of July. During the 1960s, some thought the old structure should come down, but even though the venerable hall still lacked running water and its old 1910 woodstove was an inadequate source of heat, it survived. By the 1990s, Jarbidge had made something of a comeback, boasting thirty-four permanent residents. This allowed the community to complete improvements to the building, ensuring its preservation and use into the next century.[19]

NEVADA NORTHERN RAILWAY COMPLEX

While Tonopah and Goldfield prospered, eastern Nevada experienced its own mineral boom, this one exploiting the area's copper deposits. Situated on Nevada's eastern border, White Pine County contains some of the Great Basin's most breathtaking scenery. Mineral wealth rather than natural beauty, however, originally attracted people to the region.

A flurry of gold and silver mining in White Pine County during the late 1860s gave rise to Hamilton and Treasure Hill, while a copper strike in the area founded Ely. By Nevada standards, these early discoveries were unimpressive. Hamilton and Treasure Hill declined quickly, but Ely endured. For decades, its survival was predicated more on White Pine County's livestock industry than it was on mining. Ely also benefited from the fact that Hamilton, White Pine County's original county seat, was devastated by fire in 1885. Two years later, Ely inherited the reins—and also the profits—of local government.[20]

Eastern Nevada's fortunes changed dramatically at the dawn of the twentieth century when David Bartley and Edwin Gray recognized the value of the region's copper. Although Pilot Knob and Copper Flat, lying west of Ely, had long been known to bear copper, it was not until the nation's electrical industry dramatically increased demand for the metal at the dawn of the twentieth century that the region's low-grade ore could be mined profitably. Bartley and Gray believed the area's copper supply was substantial enough to produce considerable wealth, so they persuaded some of Ely's citizens to grubstake them, and they excavated a mine. As they began to turn a profit, their mine attracted the attention of Mark Requa, who soon assumed control of the property and established the White Pine Copper Company.[21]

In 1904, Requa entered into a financial alliance with Philadelphia's Guggenheim family, which had mining interests in Utah. The Nevada Consolidated Copper Company was the result of this merger. While associated with the Guggenheims, Requa also promoted the construction of the Nevada Northern Railway. The line moved north and connected the Ely area with the Southern Pacific Railroad. It also linked the mines to the local smelter at McGill. Engaging in the monopolist tactics of the era, the Guggenheims wrested control of Nevada Consolidated from Requa and mined it in the same manner as they operated their Utah mines. Introduction of the Utah mining pattern into White Pine County profoundly influenced the development of several communities in the region as they assumed the form of company towns. The Guggenheims were not, however, the only copper barons attracted to White Pine County, and for a time several mining companies flourished in the district. During the

FACING PAGE:

TOP: The Department of the Interior recognized the Nevada Northern Railway Complex as a National Historic Landmark in 2005. The complex preserves dozens of buildings and an operating steam locomotive.

BOTTOM: The shops at the Nevada Northern Railway Complex include turn-of-the-century tools and furnishings, making the compound one of the most valuable railroad resources in the West.

1930s, the mighty Kennecott Corporation assumed control of the region's mines and dominated the area culturally, economically, and socially for more than forty years.[22]

Although copper was not as glamorous as gold and silver, extensive deposits supported communities for decades. Eventually, however, White Pine's mines succumbed to the fact that ore was not a renewable resource and prices fluctuated. During the 1970s, Kennecott began shutting down its operations. In 1983, the company closed its smelter at McGill. Although many left eastern Nevada at that time, several thousand remained long enough to witness a modest resurgence of the area's mines in the 1990s. Given the vagaries of the copper market, the residents of eastern Nevada also sought to buoy up the region's economy by developing their location's appeal as a tourist destination.[23]

When Kennecott pulled out of White Pine County, it donated the Nevada Northern railroad yards located in East Ely, along with its rolling stock and thirty-two miles of track, to the White Pine County Historical Railroad Foundation, which began restoring the facilities. The Nevada Northern Railway yard in East Ely includes more than one hundred and fifty structures. The appearance of the complex remains largely unaltered since the 1920s. Besides the multiple tracks and switches one would expect of a railroad yard, there are storage facilities, a freight house, a passenger depot, shops of various sorts, office buildings, a water tower, and a variety of other buildings and structures. In addition, the complex also houses railroad rolling stock, tools, and documents, which make this one of the best-preserved historic districts in the nation.[24]

Although most of the rail yard is strictly functional, the passenger depot is an elegant expression of period design, featuring parapets that refer to the Mission Revival style. Frederick Hale designed the two-story building, which dates to 1907, as a dramatic entrance to the complex. The real strength of the historic district lies, however, not with its few fine examples of architecture, but rather with the pristine survival of its historic resources. These monuments to Nevada's industrial past underscore the significant role the state's railroads played in its early-twentieth-century mining boom.

McGILL DEPOT

McGill, fourteen miles north of the East Ely complex, was a company town, planned and built to accommodate those who processed copper ore from local mines. In many ways, the company towns of eastern Nevada were adaptive responses on the part of industry to problems of remoteness posed by the Nevada wilderness. The copper mines were located hundreds of miles from the closest urban centers in a region that, though beautiful, was also among the most unforgiving in North America. Because the ore deposits were extensive enough to promise the support of generations of workers, the copper companies wanted to attract and sustain a stable labor force. The key to establishing workers was, of course, to entice entire families, not merely the miners themselves. Attracting families entailed supplying them with all the amenities of the nation's more settled regions, and so the companies built comfortable yet low-rent housing for their employees and supplied them with all that was required for a civilized existence.

Companies provided employees with water, garbage collection, and police and fire protection while selling commodities such as electricity, wood, and coal at reduced, subsidized prices. The companies also created opportunities for recreation and offered affordable health care. At times, they even addressed their workers' cultural needs with reading rooms and libraries and by organizing community holidays, festivals, and celebrations.[25]

Although the companies provided many of life's necessities directly to their employees, they also allowed privately owned businesses including clothing stores, meat markets, bakeries, drugstores, tobacco shops, and others into the community to cater to the full range of needs. These establishments were not directly owned by the copper companies, and they were allowed into the community only with management's approval.

The McGill Depot was a stop on the Nevada Northern Railway as it left Ely and passed north to connect with the transcontinental railroad.

Businesses had to function within social and economic constraints that the companies established. As the distinguished Nevada historian Russell R. Elliott once observed, residents of eastern Nevada's company towns "had to live within limits prescribed by company officials rather than elected officers; economic security was gained at the expense of political freedom."[26]

Because McGill was linked so completely to the copper industry, when local ore milling ended in 1983, the town lost much of its reason to exist. At this time, the fate of the McGill Depot was also called into question. The depot was built in 1910 to accommodate traffic between the company town and Ely. It features finely dressed stone block arranged in narrow and broad bands. Wide eaves designed to protect passengers from the elements are supported by knee brackets in typical depot fashion. Its shallow hipped roof includes dormers that set off the front and rail-side facades with a distinctive appearance.

The squat, plain, and functional building is not glamorous, but its role in the history of the region is not to be underestimated. It served the Nevada Northern Railway line as it headed north toward the Southern Pacific line. It was central, therefore, to the region's development. The depot's importance to the state's history was apparent to officials of the White Pine County Historical Railroad Foundation, who recognized that it could become a lineal extension of their own historic museum. They consequently adopted it and began the process of preserving the building for future generations.

MCGILL DRUGSTORE

The McGill Drugstore provides an opportunity to understand another aspect of the turn-of-the-century mining development in White Pine County. The White Pine Public Museum acquired the building in 1995 from the estate of Elsa Culbert. She and her husband, Gerald, managed the drugstore from the late 1940s until Mr. Culbert's death in 1979. As that point, his widow closed the pharmacy but maintained the business as a drugstore and soda fountain, leaving the pharmacy and its contents a relic from a previous time.[27]

The McGill Drugstore is almost as old as the community. Although its exact date of construction remains elusive, photographic evidence suggests the facility was owned by the Steptoe Drug Company at least as early as 1909. After 1915, its history is easier to trace. Documents indicate three investors acquired the property in that year and incorporated as the McGill Drug Company. A succession of owners followed, but the facility retained the same name. In 1995, supporters decided to refurbish the aged store and reopen it as a living museum. At that time, the facility was rechristened as the McGill Historical Drugstore Museum.[28]

The building's history is significant not only because it dates back to the early years of the twentieth century but also because the drugstore was one of McGill's most significant social institutions. As a company town, McGill's society was highly stratified, by class as well as by ethnicity. The economic and social barriers dividing the community were reflected in

The McGill Drugstore building dates to as early as 1909. The institution served as a pharmacy for the company town until 1979.

its physical composition. The company developed segregated residential areas within the community, isolating such groups as the Japanese, Greeks (including Serbians), and Austrians (primarily Croatians, Romanians, and Hungarians) from one another, as well as from the community's "white" population.[29] The drugstore was important to community life because its soda fountain was one of the few gathering places where everyone felt comfortable.

The building is also important for architectural reasons. The rectangular structure's corrugated-steel-on-wood-frame construction was often used in Nevada's turn-of-the-century mining towns because it was resistant to fire, a recurrent problem in the region's industrial communities. This type of building construction was functional but usually did not inspire long-term preservation. Most examples were consequently discarded over time, making the McGill building a remarkable survivor. In 1961, the front was covered with horizontal aluminum siding, diminishing the structure's integrity. The building's greatest significance, however, is in the details. A vintage oval neon "Rexall Drugs" sign hangs from the front, but in the interior one finds the most extraordinary aspect of the resource: freestanding and built-in wooden cabinets, a 1930s soda counter with stools, and a complete inventory of products and prescription records for local residents spanning decades.

MCKINLEY PARK SCHOOL

Reno's McKinley Park School represents a different side of the early-twentieth-century mining boom. The rush to Nevada and exploration for new mineral resources established camps that thrived and then faded as miners exhausted their ore. At the same time, established communities such as Reno and Elko benefited from the new flow of wealth, and residents there constructed buildings that reflected the opulence of the period. Perhaps because these towns had deeper roots, the buildings they constructed were often more elaborate and sophisticated than those emerging in their boomtown counterparts. They were, consequently, more likely to survive than the more humble structures.

Although many of Nevada's early communities had declined since the great days of the Comstock, Reno—the railroad town Charles Crocker had established at Lake's Crossing in 1869—continued to flourish. Situated on the Central Pacific line in the Truckee Meadows at the eastern edge of the Sierra Nevada, it was well positioned as a regional distribution point. A bustling, commercial city, it was not overly harmed by the Comstock's decline. It was ready to serve two decades later, therefore, as a turn-of-the-century financial hub for the Tonopah and Goldfield mining booms. Reno was also well placed to serve the construction needs of the Newlands Project, one of the Progressive Era's visionary attempts to introduce irrigation and agriculture to the arid deserts of the West. Whereas the small community of Fallon, lying about fifty miles east of Reno, was the

Reno's 1909 McKinley Park School was one of four local elementary schools known as the Spanish Quartet for their Mission Revival architecture. McKinley, one of the two survivors, now serves as a cultural center.

primary focus of project construction at the time, Reno functioned as the project's commercial and industrial supplier.[30]

Cognizant of Reno's position as Nevada's leading commercial city, progressive town elders such as Francis G. Newlands, Joseph Edward Stubbs, and H. E. Stewart worked to beautify the city. They sought to elevate its cultural tone and to construct better streets and more parks and schools.[31] It was their attempt to nourish education in the community that gave rise to the Spanish Quartet, four schools noteworthy for their elegant architecture.

George A. Ferris designed the McKinley Park School, one of two surviving examples of the Spanish Quartet. Constructed in 1909 at a cost of forty thousand dollars, it followed the pattern of the other elementary schools by drawing on Mission Revival style. It boasts a Mission Revival tower, arches, massing, and details including an elegant arcaded courtyard. Spacious classrooms allow for a maximum of natural light. Parapets adorn the wings, and the tower features Mission Revival scrolling and decoration. To further the motif of the architectural style, the brick construction is covered with stucco.[32]

The building served for decades as a striking monument to the educational ethos and aesthetic sensibilities of the Reno community during the Progressive Era. When the school reverted to the City of Reno in September 1975, the city considered demolition, but officials eventually decided the structure should become a community center. After an extensive restoration in the 1990s, the building now serves as the City of Reno's Arts and Culture Center.

BETHEL AME CHURCH

Reno's humble Bethel African Methodist Episcopal (AME) Church speaks eloquently of African Americans who confronted prejudice and challenges as they settled in the Silver State. Nevada has been called the "Mississippi of the West," and although there are many problems with this analogy, racism has been an all too prevalent theme in the state's history. In spite of numerous obstacles, African Americans played a role in northern Nevada from the start and formed part of the bedrock of Reno's society. The city's black community constructed the African Methodist Episcopal Church in 1910, and, predictably, the church became a focus of community life.

The Bethel AME Church is located between the railroad tracks and the Truckee River. In 1941, the congregation remodeled and enlarged the facility, but regardless of these changes, the importance of the building is found less in its architecture than in its history and its significance for the African American struggle in northern Nevada. The clapboard building with a gabled front originally faced the street, but in 1941 a box addition enlarged the vestibule, compromising the front elevation of the structure. In addition, workers raised the church to accommodate a full basement for a kitchen and furnace, and they clothed the original wood exterior in a brick veneer.

In 1993, the congregation moved to a new facility in Sparks, selling their original building to the Bethel Housing Development Corporation,

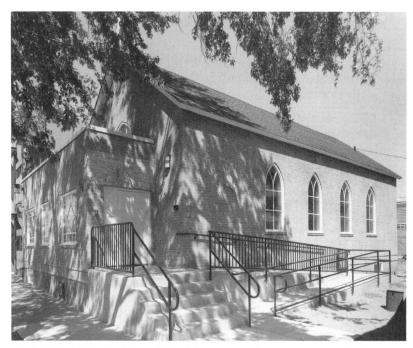

Bethel African Methodist Episcopal Church has seen many changes since its 1910 founding. When the congregation moved to a new church in 1993, the door was open for the older
facility to transform into a cultural center celebrating African American heritage in Nevada.

a nonprofit organization that used the property as a homeless shelter. A
decade later, the historic church burned, but its determined constituency
refused to let go of the building. Restoration was possible because sufficient amounts of its walls and roof had survived the fire. Using insurance
and other sources of funding, the organization reversed the damage and
diversified the institution's mandate, allowing it to host exhibits and programs focusing on African American heritage in Nevada. Although it no
longer functioned as a religious institution, the old church still represents
the longest-lived African American congregation in the state.

PIONEER BUILDING

Elko's Pioneer Building is one of Nevada's more impressive turn-of-the-century structures. In 1913, Ware and Traganza, one of the Intermountain West's leading architectural firms, designed the building to serve as office and commercial space. Its high-style design and attractive, even luxurious, interior testify to northeastern Nevada's prosperity during the Progressive Era. Elko's affluence stemmed from the exploitation of natural resources and a fortunate location placing the community on the transportation routes linking the Great Salt Lake to the communities of western Nevada and ultimately to California.

Elko County includes more than seventeen thousand square miles in the state's northeastern corner. Larger than Massachusetts, Rhode Island, and Connecticut combined, the county boasts the beautiful Ruby Mountains, the striking Jarbidge Range, and thousands of acres of high-desert terrain. The Humboldt River and its tributaries provide water for much of Elko County, and as early as the 1850s, ranchers used the region to pasture livestock, anticipating the future importance of agriculture for the area.[33] Elko County was also blessed with rich mineral deposits. During the nineteenth century, the strike at Tuscarora along with a series of less important mineral discoveries contributed to the region's economic development. Whereas the county's mineral wealth fueled the economy and filled the coffers of local government, the county's sustained growth was due largely to the development of its livestock industry and to its intermediary position along the intercontinental railroad.

The town of Elko was, in fact, a creation of the Central Pacific Railroad. Rushing its way across Nevada, the transcontinental line reached Elko in 1869. A few months earlier, Charles Crocker, the ubiquitous railroad magnate, had selected the site as a division point and named it Elko. At that time, Crocker's new town was situated in Lander County, an enormous expanse of land representing nearly a quarter of the state's total area. Austin, the Lander County seat, was too far removed from Elko to serve the young community's governmental needs, so the state legislature redrew Nevada's map and created Elko County, naming it after the railroad town.[34]

In the 1870s, the town of Elko emerged as the area's commercial, governmental, and cultural center. During the twentieth century, the community's fate would continue to rise and fall with its mining industry, but railroading and ranching always provided a stabilizing counterbalance for its economy. Beginning in the 1960s, northeastern Nevada added a new chapter to its mining heritage with the discovery and development of the famed Carlin Trend, a vast stretch of ore containing microscopic gold, roughly five miles wide and forty miles long, extending across north-central Nevada. The trend's mines transformed contemporary Nevada into one of the world's premier centers of gold production and energized the society and culture of Elko County. One of Elko's most remarkable cultural assets is the internationally known Western Folklife Center, which was organized in 1980 and is housed in the Pioneer Building.

The four-story U-shaped Arts and Crafts structure originally featured an exterior ceramic-tile frieze that separated the main floor of commercial space from the offices upstairs. The building is particularly noteworthy for its Pioneer Bar, taken from the Pioneer Saloon, which began operating at the site in 1868. It is a remarkable, extensive wood and leaded-glass bar that provides a focal point for the center's entertainment today, just as it did a hundred years ago for the bar's first clientele. The newly restored saloon also features well-appointed, ornate details and finish work.

In its early years, the Pioneer Building housed upscale shops and a café on its ground floor, while its upper floors provided space for the offices of a livestock company, a judge, and a social club. Over the years the Pioneer's uses changed, paralleling economic and social transformations occurring in downtown Elko. The structure's upper floors were converted into apartments and then into hotel rooms. By the 1970s, the shops and businesses on the building's ground level were catering to the less prosperous members of the community. In the early 1980s, attempts to convert the Pioneer into a casino, a hotel, and finally a striptease bar all failed.

In 1991, George Gund III, a member of the Western Folklife Center's Board of Trustees, decided that problems facing the Pioneer Building and the center might have a common solution. The center required space for its programs, exhibits, and administrative offices while the historic structure's commercial fortunes had declined. So Gund purchased the building and donated it to the organization. The following year, the Western Folklife Center moved into the Pioneer and began its restoration. After many incarnations, this remarkable monument to Elko's prosperous Progressive Era had begun a new life that would carry it into the next century.

FACING PAGE:
Elko's Pioneer Building dates to 1913 and now serves as home to the internationally famous Annual Cowboy Poetry Festival.

OATS PARK SCHOOL

The growth and prosperity of northern Nevada's agricultural communities during the Progressive Era are documented by that period's schoolhouses. Throughout the region, a farsighted, optimistic spirit manifested in well-designed, architecturally interesting monuments to public education. Because of the care people took in building these schools, many remain and are often counted among northern Nevada's longest-lived and best-loved structures.

Fallon's Oats Park School, one of the oldest surviving buildings in the community, ranks among these revered relics of the past. When the school was completed in 1915, it had been only about a dozen years since the town was hardly more than Mike Fallon's little store on his ranch property in the arid Carson Sink. In the intervening decade, the town grew dramatically due to the Newlands Reclamation Project and became the seat of Churchill County. Thanks largely to the efforts of Nevada congressman Francis G. Newlands, Congress established the U.S. Reclamation Service in 1902 and entrusted it with the mission of reclaiming desert lands through irrigation. That same year, the Reclamation Service launched a project in the Fallon area designed to irrigate thousands of acres of desert, by channeling water from the Truckee and Carson rivers.[35] With access to water, Fallon's population began to swell, and by 1914, it needed to construct a new elementary school.

The community decided to erect the school at the edge of Oats Park on the east side of town, and it asked Frederic DeLongchamps to design the structure. Reno contractors Friedhoff and Hoeffel, who had recently completed a grammar school in Yerington, built the facility in Fallon with a budget of twenty thousand dollars. DeLongchamps designed a simple two-level building. It was distinguished, nonetheless, by an attractive Neoclassical Revival pedimented pavilion located in the center of its main facade. In 1921, the school district enlarged the Oats Park facility with north and south wings. Because DeLongchamps designed the additions, his plan preserved the integrity of his initial design. Originally, the front

The Oats Park School in Fallon is one of many monumental structures designed by Nevada's renowned architect, Frederic DeLongchamps. The building opened in 1915.

entrance featured an ornate vestibule entrance with pilasters surmounted by a beautiful half-circle fanlight with ornate trim in cast cement and brick. Sometime after 1953 and possibly in response to a 1954 earthquake, this detail was lost behind a new plain facade.

The Oats Park School served the children of Fallon for more than fifty years. In the 1970s, the Churchill County School District built a new grammar school, and the sturdy old structure was put to other uses. In the 1990s, the old school transformed into a community theater, and the building was returned to its formal glory. It stands today as a beautiful architectural statement, reminding visitors of the vibrancy of Nevada's cultural life during the Progressive Era.[36]

FERNLEY EAST END SCHOOL

Fernley also owes its early good fortune to the Newlands Project, which envisioned transforming the central Nevada desert into an oasis. The most prominent community to emerge from the project was Fallon, but the entire region benefited as well. Fernley was a small settlement lying on the edge of Nevada's infamous Forty-Mile Desert when the Newlands Project began. As it progressed, the area's desert lands realized a new potential because of the introduction of water. With the arriving families, the need for a school was quickly apparent.

The East End School dates to 1910 and was constructed on the J. Richard McColloch ranch, to the east of Fernley. The humble building lacked the grandeur of other schools dating to this period, but it fulfilled the

The humble East End School in Fernley was built in 1910 and then moved to its current location in 1932.

needs of the Fernley area for a dozen years until a new structure replaced it in 1922. After standing empty for a decade, the schoolhouse found a new purpose when the Fernley Ladies Aid Society purchased it in 1932. They subsequently had the old school moved to the center of town, covered with a coat of stucco, and placed into community service. Among its new func tions, it was to serve as a local church, since Fernley's limited population, ranging from four hundred to five hundred during the 1920s and 1930s, could not afford religious structures for the various denominations. The old school subsequently provided space for several congregations.

Originally, the school was a simple clapboard-sided building with a steeply pitched roof surmounted by a small cupola above the front entrance. After the move to downtown Fernley, the building was elongated with an addition to the rear and an open vestibule enclosing the entry. What had been an enclosed cupola was replaced by an open belfry. It is an unassuming building for a small town, but its various uses for decades have made it a central part of community life in Fernley.

YERINGTON GRAMMAR SCHOOL

Whereas Fernley and Fallon developed in response to the Newlands Project primarily as agricultural communities, Lyon County's growth was dependent upon the development of both its ranching and its mining, echoing a pattern found in Elko, to the northeast. Lands lying along the Walker River east of Carson Valley proved suitable for agriculture and attracted early settlement. The community of Yerington, set today among the blue-green alfalfa fields of Mason Valley, dates to 1859. At that time, N. A. H. "Hock" Mason founded the first ranch in the valley, giving it his name. The following year, the U.S. Army established Fort Churchill north of Mason Valley. For decades, farming and ranching prospered in the region. Its agricultural wealth even attracted the vast Miller and Lux Corporation to the area. In the first decade of the twentieth century, this enormous cattle and meatpacking operation centered in California held land in three states, dominating the Pacific Coast's meat markets. Due to

Architects C. D. McDonald and J. J. Beatty designed the Yerington Grammar School, which dates to the second decade of the twentieth century.

its association with Mason, the corporation purchased land in Mason Valley, and for a time integrated it into its vast industrial operations.[37]

In 1911, while Miller and Lux was still operating in the valley, Yerington became the seat of Lyon County, taking the honor from Dayton. A year later, the area experienced a copper boom. Although prospectors had discovered the mineral there during the 1860s, as in eastern Nevada, miners did not exploit the ore until the twentieth century. Copper mining continued in Mason Valley for several decades, and in the 1940s, the powerful Anaconda Company purchased the area's leading mine. The copper boom ended shortly after World War I, but mining resumed for three decades beginning in the 1950s. Anaconda sold its Lyon County copper mine in the 1980s, and its great open pit changed hands several times. Although copper mining continued on a more modest scale, the great Anaconda pit was finally abandoned in 2000.[38] Although Yerington's long association with mining was crucial to the community's development, its agricultural heritage has played a more significant role in shaping its culture and identity.

At the beginning of the twentieth century, an expanding economy and a rapidly increasing population required the construction of a new school. In 1911, the town began building Yerington Grammar School no. 9, located at the intersection of California and Littel streets, two blocks off Main. Reflecting the Progressive Era's commitment to investing in the education of its youth, the community hired two Reno architects, C. D. McDonald and J. J. Beatty, to design the $16,600 building. Reno contractors Friedhoff and Hoeffel, who two years later would build the Oats Park School, constructed the stylish two-and-a-half-story structure to accommodate one hundred children. The lower floor is composed of rusticated concrete blocks, providing a foundation for the main body of the school, composed of finely pressed brick from Colorado. The building's facade is elaborate, featuring balanced pedimented gables over two projecting bays, and a smaller gable crowning the main entrance, which supports a cupola with a bell-cast roof.[39]

In 1935, the handsome structure was enlarged according to plans drafted by DeLongchamps, preserving the stylish look of the building. The structure continued to function as Yerington's elementary school until 1980. The schoolhouse's years of service inspired a group of local people led by the late Jeanne Dini to initiate the Yerington Grammar School no. 9 Restoration Project in the 1990s. Hoping to provide their community with a much needed arts complex, the group restored the old grammar school and transformed it into the Yerington Cultural Center.

DOUGLAS COUNTY HIGH SCHOOL

An early leader in Nevada's agricultural industry, Douglas County prospered in the first decades of the twentieth century. Whereas Genoa had been the center of the Carson Valley economy, society, and local government in the 1860s, fortunes shifted in 1906 when the Virginia and Truckee

Railroad extended a line to the middle of the county. With an inexpensive means to transport produce to distant markets, agriculture prospered and the towns of Minden and Gardnerville grew.

By the second decade of the century, it became clear that the Douglas County seat should shift from Genoa to the emerging population center. The transfer stalled because neither Minden nor Gardnerville was quick to yield the honor of becoming the location of county government. Eventually, residents of the two towns reached a compromise, which gave Minden the courthouse and Gardnerville a new high school. In 1915, the Nevada legislature authorized funding for both structures, and Frederic J. DeLongchamps was called into service, once again, to design the two facilities.[40]

The Douglas County High School, designed by Frederic DeLongchamps, now serves as a museum and cultural center.

The Neoclassical high school was constructed of "sturdy brick" and offered ample space for a growing student body. It was ornamented with six Doric columns on a central porch. An iron entablature featured a cornice articulated with dentils. The symmetrical brick building includes a main floor with a full basement. Like the stylish McKinley Park School, the Oats Park School, and Yerington Grammar School no. 9, the Douglas County facility reflects the values of the Progressive Era and the faith of people in their region.

When a new high school was constructed in 1958, the DeLongchamps structure became the local middle school, and it served the community in that capacity for another quarter century. During the mid-1980s, however, new earthquake building codes forced local officials to declare the school unsafe. Confronted with the cost of a complete seismic retrofit for the structure, the local school board moved the middle school elsewhere and reluctantly considered demolishing the old building. Eventually, however, the community saved the building and placed it into service as a museum.

LAS VEGAS SPRINGS PRESERVE

Although the uninitiated often conclude that Las Vegas began with the birth of the Strip after the Second World War, the roots of the community are deep, and as in northern Nevada, the region's agricultural potential was central to its early development. As noted in chapter 1, the springs, situated in the heart of the Las Vegas Valley, attracted Native Americans to the region for millennia prior to the advent of Euro-Americans. Archaeological evidence indicates the Anasazi, Patayan, and Southern Paiutes used the springs on a seasonal basis for centuries, harvesting vegetation sustained by the water to augment their food supply, and by hunting local wildlife. In historic times, Mexican explorers and traders watered at the springs on their way from New Mexico to California, and mountain men and military explorers from the United States also visited the oasis when they traversed the region. The best known of these was Capt. John C. Frémont, who led a topographical expedition into the Las Vegas Valley in

1844. His team charted one of the New Mexicans' caravan routes through
Nevada, mapped it, and, in accordance with New Mexican tradition, called
it the Spanish Trail. It became one of the main routes into southern California during the middle decades of the nineteenth century.[41]

In the last half of the nineteenth century, the springs continued to
play a pivotal role in the history of the Las Vegas Valley. Whereas the early
Euro-American explorers and traders who crossed the region did not settle there, the Mormons who arrived in 1855 did in fact establish the area's
first settlement. After the Mormons were called back to Utah in 1857, the
ranchers who followed them into the valley established businesses near
the life-giving water of the Las Vegas Valley's springs.

People came and went, but water was a constant, and without it, trails
would have led elsewhere. Because of this, no site in the Las Vegas Valley is more important to local history than the Las Vegas Springs. Eventually, the natural sources of water attracted Senator William A. Clark of
Montana, who was driving his San Pedro, Los Angeles, and Salt Lake Railroad through the valley in 1905, the year the company platted the town of
Las Vegas as a division point for the line. At the same time, Clark and his
associates founded the Las Vegas Valley Land and Water Company, which
began to monopolize the distribution of local springwater.

The water company constructed several buildings at the site known as
Big Springs, and among these was the Little Springs Spring House, constructed in 1917. The building was intended to protect the main source
of water from contamination by livestock and by people swimming in
it. When it was originally constructed, it had a flat roof. In 1926, it was
improved with the addition of a shallow gabled roof. This is a simple,
functional structure, built so low to the ground that it is easily overlooked.
The building serves as a reminder that people erect many sorts of structures and that function typically defined form. The Spring House was not
intended to outlive its use, but it did. The building survived silently to witness the dramatic growth of the community and the metamorphosis of the
privately controlled Las Vegas Valley Land and Water Company into the
publicly operated Las Vegas Valley Water District.

The springs in the Las Vegas Valley have attracted settlement and visitors for millennia. Part of the rich legacy there includes shallow structures designed to protect the natural sources of water.

There were attempts during the 1970s and the 1980s to use the spring site for purposes that would have destroyed the historic value of centuries-old archaeological remnants and buildings dating to the dawn of the valley's historic period. In 1988, local residents forced design changes in a flood-control project that, if left unaltered, would have obliterated a site reaching back to some of the oldest habitation of the region. In that same year, the rare Las Vegas bear poppy was discovered at the springs. The Las Vegas Valley Water District began working to preserve the area and to use it as a means for educating the public on the importance of water conservation. The agency established the Las Vegas Springs Archaeological Site, organized a board of trustees to oversee its operations, and began working to create a cultural and environmental center. This effort gave rise to the Las Vegas Springs Preserve, an organization committed to preserving the cultural, biological, and water resources at the Las Vegas Springs Archaeological Site. The Little Springs Spring House reminds visitors of the intimate link existing between water resources and human settlement in the history of the arid Southwest.

LAS VEGAS RAILROAD COTTAGES

The 1905 platting of the Las Vegas town site set the stage for a broad range of changes besides the development of a water system. The population explosion in southern Nevada ensued as the door opened for hundreds to settle there, and new arrivals needed housing. Within a few years, sixty-four modest bungalow-like houses were erected near the railroad depot in specifically designated residential blocks.

Constructed between 1909 and 1912, these homes followed a similar form, which can be classified as pyramidal cottages. They were one-story with hipped roofs ending in flared, boxed eaves and square brackets. Stucco covered cinder-block walls, offering insulation for early residents before the invention of air-conditioning. Porches featured railing with spare balustrades.

After the 1905 platting of the Las Vegas town site, simple houses, known as railroad cottages, filled many of the residential blocks. Few survived into the twenty-first century.

The first houses in a community, whether in seventeen-century New England or in Las Vegas at the beginning of the twentieth century, are typically modest, quickly erected, and not necessarily intended to last. Usually, they do not survive long as ambitions exceed the practical, small scale of a former time. As later booms brought hundreds of thousands to southern Nevada and the value of real estate shifted from thousands of dollars to millions, the railroad cottages became anachronistic, run-down nuisances occupying land promising wealth. Ultimately, most were demolished, but one found its way to the Clark County Museum, where it survives as a relic of the early twentieth century. Others moved to the Springs Preserve, where they will also help in the interpretation of the past.[42]

THE RAILROAD COTTAGES and the Little Springs Spring House recall a time when Las Vegas, modern Nevada's largest and most celebrated city, was first established. These resources are simple, vernacular structures, serving the basic needs of the railroad town that generated them. More often, however, the state's turn-of-the-century buildings reflect an increasing sophistication. The gold and silver rushes of the 1860s sparked Nevada's development, but most of its settlements were meager, with modest architecture that was cheap, fast, and expedient. The mining rushes of the early twentieth century similarly spawned short-lived boom-towns with pragmatic, humble architecture, but the extraordinary wealth of some of these strikes also gave rise to desert metropolises, boasting sophisticated buildings with high-style architectural designs. When Nevada's Progressive Era miners exhausted local ore deposits, however, even these communities proved to be as ephemeral as the proud cities of the Comstock era. Nevada's mighty mountain ranges and its forbidding desert landscape, the backdrop for this flurry of mining excitement, were affected but hardly tamed by this second great influx of immigrants into the state's domain.

5 After the Boom

The 1920s introduced yet another phase of history and economic change in Nevada's social and cultural life, lasting into the 1930s. This was an era of cultural experimentation and economic challenges, and a new generation of Nevadans followed an established pattern of finding innovative ways to thrive. While gaming and the divorce industry contributed to the state's economy, Nevadans learned to turn their Wild West image into a tourist attraction. At the same time, enterprising innkeepers, appealing to the divorce trade, cultivated a sophisticated and urbane environment for their long-term guests. Twelve historic buildings document this dynamic period of growth and diversification in the state's social and cultural life. People have only recently begun to regard many of the buildings of this exciting era as historic. Although the resources could easily have been demolished, local groups have transformed them into cornerstones of the Nevada cultural map.

MARVEL RANCH COOKHOUSE

Midway across Nevada on the transcontinental railroad and Highway 80, Battle Mountain provides a rest along the expanse. It is a place of eco-

The Marvel Ranch cookhouse, built in 1920, is an excellent expression of the type of architecture that once dominated the rural parts of the state.

nomic variations, grounded in the twin industries of ranching and min-ing. Battle Mountain takes its name from one of two early engagements between local Shoshone and emigrants. The name subsequently became associated with the range and then with a mining district, organized in 1866. With the arrival of the transcontinental railroad in 1868, a nearby community that was known as Battle Mountain shifted to its present loca-tion to take advantage of the benefits of rail-based commerce.[1]

Unfortunately for Battle Mountain, nearby mines were rarely as prof-itable as they were elsewhere in the state, and the community spent decades competing, unsuccessfully, for a stature similar to that of Elko to the east and Winnemucca to the west on the railroad. Instead, the latter two succeeded in capturing much of the regional commerce, leaving Battle Mountain to struggle economically. Nevertheless, the town maintained a fairly stable existence, and when the mines of Austin, the seat of county government to the south, failed, Battle Mountain began to call for a shift to the north. After years of defending itself, Austin finally lost the seat of Lander County to Battle Mountain in an election in 1979.[2]

The Marvel cookhouse was part of the 25 Ranch operated by the locally well-known Marvel family. It is an excellent expression of a way of life that typifies the clichéd image of the West as seen by most of the world. Although the ranch was established in the nineteenth century, the cook-house dates to 1920. The two-story building is simple and functional. Its gable front has eave returns and a porch, recalling classical design, but its unornamented treatment speaks to the functional origin of the structure. At some point, the porch was screened to provide additional protected space. The Marvel family donated its cookhouse to the Lander County Historical Society, to be moved into Battle Mountain so it could serve the community as a place to interpret local ranching heritage.

PERSHING COUNTY COURTHOUSE

To the west of Battle Mountain, the town of Lovelock also struggled in com-petition with more prosperous neighbors on the transcontinental rail-road. In this case, Winnemucca to the northeast and Reno to the southwest eclipsed the financial fortunes of Lovelock, with its economy sustained largely by agriculture. Nevertheless, the community proved its mettle by surviving and, in fact, prospering during the early twentieth century. Ultimately, Lovelock benefited from a peculiar set of circumstances that conspired to create one of Nevada's most remarkable courthouses and its youngest county, the one named after Gen. John J. "Blackjack" Pershing, commander of the American forces during World War I.

Throughout the nineteenth and early twentieth centuries, Hum-boldt County managed a huge amount of land in north-central Nevada. Among the communities in the county was Lovelock, a smaller rival of Winnemucca, the seat of government to the north. When the Hum-boldt County Courthouse burned in 1918, the residents of Lovelock were uninterested in helping to foot the bill for a new public structure in Winnemucca. They consequently petitioned the Nevada legislature for the formation of a new county carved from the southern half of Humboldt County, a request honored in 1919.

The creation of Pershing County fostered competition between adja-cent communities that both needed new courthouses, Winnemucca to replace the burned structure, and Lovelock to provide a facility for the new local government. Both turned to Frederic DeLongchamps, the Reno architect who had earned a solid reputation with his previous courthouses and numerous other public and private buildings. For Winnemucca, DeLongchamps was able to employ ample funds in the design of one of the grandest county edifices in the state.

If it had been simply a financial contest, smaller Lovelock was destined to lose. Indeed, the newly elected Pershing County commissioners rejected another architect's plan for a conventional courthouse on a

The 1920 Pershing County Courthouse is remarkable for its round shape. DeLongchamps patterned it after Thomas Jefferson's library at the University of Virginia, inspired in turn by the Pantheon in Rome.

scale much smaller than its northern neighbor. They subsequently asked DeLongchamps to provide something different. The response was a design that sets the structure apart from others in the state as well as the nation. DeLongchamps drew inspiration from Thomas Jefferson's design for the library at the University of Virginia. Echoed in the round dome of Monticello, Jefferson's structure paid tribute to the Pantheon, a pre-Christian temple in Rome. This classical religious edifice later served as a church, but it stood apart from its contemporaries because of its round shape. Jefferson was certainly drawn to the unusual design, understanding that it would make his library unique, but the symbolism was also deliberate: a structure dedicated to Roman gods and then the Christian Deity came to honor the written word, as though the intellect were divine in itself, by housing the university's collection of books. For Jefferson, the new Republic was not to be founded on religion but rather on knowledge.

When DeLongchamps borrowed the design for the 1920 Pershing County Courthouse, the emphasis shifted to pay homage to justice and the democracy Jefferson had helped to establish. The innovative nature of this adaptation is demonstrated by the fact that a nationwide survey revealed no other historic round courthouses. The fact that Lovelock erected its courthouse more than a decade before John Russell Pope submitted his similar design for the Jefferson Memorial in Washington, D.C., underscores how innovative DeLongchamps was when he looked to Jefferson's work for inspiration.[3]

Not surprisingly, the residents of Lovelock have taken a great deal of pride in the courthouse since its construction. It is far smaller than its more expensive and ornate counterpart in Winnemucca, but the Pershing County facility stands apart from all the rest simply because of its shape. Unfortunately, the local custodians painted the round, domed ceiling of the courtroom at the beginning of the twenty-first century, replacing the classical off-white with a gaudy portrait of the sky, complete with clouds and the cliché of a soaring eagle. Paint, however, is reversible, and one can hope that the dignity of this nationally significant space can be restored.

CALIENTE DEPOT

In southern Nevada, another small railroad town found itself easily eclipsed by a growing giant. Caliente was designated as a stop on a railroad line that would extend north from the Las Vegas Valley. At the turn of the century when the railroad was being planned, there was no reason to imagine that the future town of Las Vegas would prove mightier than Caliente. It was only clear that both locations would prove to be good places for stops on the line.

Platted in 1901, Caliente took its name from a nearby hot spring. A newcomer for Lincoln County, the town occupies the juncture of Clover Creek and Meadow Valley Wash. Its origin recalls a fierce competition between the San Pedro, Los Angeles, and Salt Lake Railroad and the Union Pacific. The dispute resulted in violent conflict on the ground and legal wrangling in the courtroom. By 1902, the parties signed a joint ownership agreement, but even before then, Caliente took shape, anticipating expanding business and the arrival of residents as the railroad, regardless of who was in charge, passed through the valley.[4]

With a population of more than two thousand by the end of the first decade of the twentieth century, Caliente was larger than many other com-

The 1923 Mission Revival Caliente Depot was the design of the acclaimed Los Angeles firm of John and Donald Parkinson.

munities on the line, including Las Vegas to the south. This, however, was only a temporary situation. Flooding damaged the track, and other issues drove away many of the residents until the community stabilized at a little more than one thousand people.

Caliente's two-story 1923 depot is in the Mission Revival style, then popular in the American Southwest. The prolific father-and-son Los Angeles firm of John and Donald Parkinson provided the plans, giving tiny Caliente one of the most prestigious and monumental expressions of architecture in the state. The largest of the early buildings in town, the depot served as a division-office complex for the railroad, and as a hotel and restaurant for travelers, in addition to the normal depot duties. The design included scrolled towering parapets, arcades with rows of rounded arches and pillars, a stucco finish, and a red-tile roof.

The hotel part of the depot closed before World War II, and the place ceased to house a division office with the change from labor-intensive steam to diesel after the war. In 1970, the railroad leased the building to the city, which moved into the empty space. At that time, some envisioned the large facility serving as a museum, library, and arts center, an idea the community slowly implemented over the subsequent years.

WASHOE COUNTY LIBRARY, SPARKS BRANCH

Sparks was established in 1905, the same year as Las Vegas, and like its southern Nevada counterpart, Caliente, and like Lovelock to the north, Sparks was organized as a railroad stop. Originally, the Central Pacific had used Wadsworth, east of the Truckee Meadows, as the main division point. After the turn of the century, the Southern Pacific Railroad, which had assumed control of the line, reworked much of the track, abandoning Wadsworth. The railroad subsequently selected the sparsely inhabited ranch land east of Reno along the Truckee River to serve as the new division point. The town was named after the popular contemporary Nevada governor, John Sparks.[5]

It had been easy for Reno, far larger than all its neighbors, to dominate

Frederic DeLongchamps designed the first branch of the Washoe County Library in Sparks. It opened in 1931.

Washoe County, but Sparks, though always a smaller sibling, demanded its own services. In 1931, Washoe County opened its first branch library in Sparks. Frederic DeLongchamps designed the Mediterranean Revival structure, which was distinguished by a red-tile roof and a distinctive entry way. Twin staircases converge above a doorway to the basement. The main floor entryway has a striking rounded arch protecting double doors, surmounted by a semicircular transom window. Lanterns decorate either side of the doorway.

Rowse and Belz Contractors constructed the brick building, with a Flemish bond, featuring dark-red headers contrasting with lighter-red stretchers—a favorite motif of DeLongchamps. Brick quoins at the corners and a wide brick belt course between the basement and main floor provide additional accents. The building cost less than twenty thousand dollars and survives as the oldest government building in the community.[6]

In 1965, the Sparks library became the Sparks Judicial Court. Three decades later, the building was ready for a new use. In 1993, the city transferred the building to the Sparks Heritage Foundation and Museum, which turned it into a cultural center.

CALIFORNIA BUILDING

One of the challenges of the twentieth century was to bind far-flung communities together with roads for automobiles to augment or in some cases to replace the nineteenth-century system of railroads. The Lincoln Highway passing through Ely, Eureka, Austin, and Fallon, and the Victory Highway, taking a northerly route, tied the state together with other parts of the nation. To celebrate this early success in the development of the North American continent, Reno hosted a Transcontinental Highway

The State of California funded a building for Reno's Idlewild Park. Known as the California Building, it was part of the Transcontinental Highway Exposition of 1927 in celebration of the completion of the Lincoln and Victory highways.

Exposition situated on the western, upstream, part of the Truckee River in 1927. California donated a handsome Mission Revival structure to house exhibits for the celebration. Few along the new highway routes failed to recognize the potential for tourism and commerce, and Californians were eager to make certain Nevadans understood the connection the new highway afforded.

The California Building also served as a war memorial to casualties of the First World War. Funding from the California legislature included the dedication, "To the memory of those who gave the last full measure of devotion to this nation." A plaque on the outside of the building remains as a testimony to that sentiment. The building was consequently presented to the Darrell Dunkle American Legion Post no. 1, which then transferred ownership to the City of Reno in 1938. Eventually, the California Building became the principal indoor facility in Idlewild Park.[7]

The exterior of the California Building is treated with beige stucco on wood lath. The north elevation features the main entrance, framed with three large round-arched openings supported by four piers. A Mission Revival bell tower, including a faux decorative bell, caps the east elevation. One of the more remarkable features of the building is an eight-foot round window, which dominates the western elevation. Because the opening splays outward, the feature is even more dramatic when seen from the outside. The building is capped with a red-tile roof. Its commodious auditorium has been a favorite location for special events since it opened. The heavy timbers of the truss system are exposed, and a large fireplace dominates the interior. The use of the building has changed little in eighty years, accommodating a wide variety of meetings and events.

RIVERSIDE HOTEL

Located downstream from the California Building, in the heart of downtown Reno, the Riverside Hotel represents an important part of the Truckee River Arts and Culture District. The structure stands on the site of three earlier hotels. Charles William Fuller of Sierra County, California, erected the first building there. Beginning in 1859, Fuller constructed a bridge across the Truckee and built an adjacent log structure for shelter. In 1861, he sold the bridge and building to Myron C. Lake. After that, the bridge was known as Lake's Crossing. In 1862, Lake erected an inn on the site of Fuller's original structure and called it Lake House. After Lake's death in 1884, a subsequent owner, Harry Gosse, constructed the first brick Riverside Hotel on the site, but it was gutted by fire in 1922. In 1926, George Wingfield acquired the property and commissioned Frederic DeLongchamps to design the third Riverside Hotel, which stands today. Wingfield had made a fortune during the turn-of-the-century gold rush to central Nevada. By the 1920s, he had transformed his wealth into a banking and investment empire that dominated the state's economy and political scene.

DeLongchamps designed the impressive six-story Riverside Hotel in the Late Gothic Revival style. The reinforced concrete building was clothed in brick and terra-cotta finish work. Store fronts filled the ground floor. Matching five-story bays on the east and north elevations, covered

with cream-colored, terra-cotta details, provide some of the more striking architectural elements of the building. The motif achieves its decorative climax at the roofline, where terra-cotta filigree rises to a parapet with
Gothic arches filled with a floral-paneled frieze. The building included
corner suites with living room and bedroom, kitchen, and dining room.
To accommodate long-term guests, each suite had a refrigerator and elec-
tric range.[8]

Wingfield, one of Nevada's more controversial figures, planned to rent
the Riverside's rooms to people who were visiting the state to take advantage of its liberal divorce laws. For many years, the hotel sustained itself on
this trade, situated as it was next door to the Washoe County Courthouse.
As casino gaming developed in Nevada during the 1940s and 1950s, a section of the Riverside's first floor was converted into a casino. In addition, a
west wing was added to the hotel in 1950. During this period, the Riverside
became one of northern Nevada's best-known nightspots, its theater-
restaurant featuring big-name entertainers such as Frank Sinatra, Frankie
Lane, the Mills Brothers, Danny Kaye, Jimmy Durante, Nat "King" Cole,
and Rosemary Clooney.

By the 1970s, changes in other states' divorce laws had made it easier
for people to obtain legal separations elsewhere, and the old hotel began
to decline. A succession of owners failed to make the property thrive over
the long term. In 1987, increasing debt finally forced its doors closed, an
elegant reminder of a past time of prosperity. When it seemed certain the
property would be demolished in the late 1990s, a plan emerged to restore
the facility. The hotel now provides housing for artists and space for businesses. The ground floor thrives with a restaurant, a coffee shop, and gallery space.

FACING PAGE:
Reno's Riverside Hotel stands on the site of a line of predecessors that dates back to 1862.
Frederic DeLongchamps designed the 1926 building that still stands on the south bank
of the Truckee River.

GALENA CREEK FISH HATCHERY

For all the development in the Truckee Meadows, one of the greatest assets of the community has been its surrounding wilderness. The Galena Creek Fish Hatchery represents an effort to make amends after a growing population ravaged the region's ecosystem in the 1860s and 1870s. Fisheries decimated local streams and lakes to feed a growing population, providing restaurants with ample supplies of trout. When restocking became an important goal in the early twentieth century, Washoe County opened hatcheries to raise trout. The hatchery at Galena Creek reflects a trend, which began in the 1920s, to combine habitat conservation and recreational development. Washoe County paid $8,310 to Wine and Williams, building contractors, to build the facility in 1931. A New Deal project added to the facility in the late 1930s. The fish hatchery operated until 1949, augmenting the main county fish hatchery on the Truckee River in Reno.

Situated at sixty-four hundred feet above sea level, within the pine forest of the Mount Rose Highway, the Galena Creek Fish Hatchery was exposed to harsh winter conditions. It is a simple, utilitarian structure built on a platform created by stone walls on the down slope to provide a building surface overlooking a steeply sided ravine. Galena Creek flows below, furnishing the fresh water for the cultivation of trout, raised to stock Nevada's streams. A concrete foundation supports thick random-course stone walls for the stout rectangular building. Ocular windows at the gables and sturdy stone buttresses at the corners provide additional style for the simple structure.

The facility suffered flood damage in 1949, and the county subsequently ceased operating the hatchery. The Boy Scouts, Camp Fire Girls, Sierra Sage Council of Camp Fire, and Washoe Bowmen and Sierra Archers subsequently used the site. In 1956, the Boy Scouts added a large stone fireplace to furnish heat in cold winters for the 3,750 square feet of the interior. In 1994, Washoe County regained control of the property, which the agency then incorporated into the Galena Creek Regional Park.

The Galena Creek Fish Hatchery was one of several similar facilities scattered throughout the eastern slope of the Sierra. Dating to 1931, the building spawned fish for transplant into Nevada's rivers and lakes.

Unfortunately, the building's roof failed after successive winters of heavy snow. A modern restoration installed a new roof system that sensitively rests on steel pillars, sparing the old walls the burden of a new roof. In 2006, the hatchery reopened to the public, serving a wide variety of special events for the park.

EUREKA HIGH SCHOOL

Along the route of the Lincoln Highway, in the center of the state, quiet Eureka slumbers where mines once made the place teem with prosperity. Dating to the first period of mineral exploration in the state, Eureka was originally part of a mining district that was something of a satellite to Austin, managed as it was by Lander County. The success of the new mining district allowed Eureka County to separate from its parent in 1873.

Eureka and the new county thrived longer than most mining districts, thanks to an extensive, moderately valued ore body that was sufficient to keep employment steady for years. Eventually, however, the mines closed, leaving the isolated community with little means of support. As a county seat, Eureka did manage to retain government as a local industry. In 1923, circumstances allowed for the erection of a new public school to serve all grades. It eventually functioned exclusively as the high school.

The two-story brick structure has a pronounced fluted cornice along its flat roof, a detail in keeping with the Art Deco style popular at the time. Rows of square four-pane windows dominate the two floors of the front elevation. A staircase rises to a front door framed by a classical cornice and two pairs of pilasters.

The Eureka school closed in the mid-1990s, but the old building lingered, as schools often do, tugging at the heartstrings of those who attended the facility. Support for the high school inspired some to seek funding for a study of the building. Nevertheless, the fate of the building remains in question.

LATTER-DAY SAINTS STAKE TABERNACLE IN ELY

Still farther to the east along the Lincoln Highway, Ely was enjoying the benefits of the new connection with the outside world, augmenting the Nevada Northern Railway. Just as the highway was opening in 1927, the Church of Jesus Christ of Latter-day Saints built a brick stake tabernacle in Ely. The importance of that faith early in the region dates to a time when much of eastern Nevada was part of Utah. Because the Mormon Church discouraged mining at the time, mineral discoveries inspired Congress to remove two longitudinal degrees of western Utah to be appended to Nevada, a pro-mining state.[9] The architect for the Ely stake tabernacle is unknown, but the design incorporates elements of Colonial Revival, making the building a stately if somewhat restrained presence in the community. The contractor was Joseph Van Carolos Young, grandson of early church leader Brigham Young.

TOP: The Eureka High School dates to 1923. It closed in the 1990s, and its fate remains in question.

BOTTOM: The Church of Jesus Christ of Latter-day Saints Stake Tabernacle in Ely opened in 1927 and now serves as home to the White Pine Community Choir Association.

The two-story building has an imposing front elevation soaring to the point of a gable end with eave returns in keeping with classical architecture. Quoins are achieved with alternating brick and concrete. The doorway includes a large Palladian arch capped by a hexagonal window. Elsewhere, the cornice features dentils.

The church is an expression of a ten-year program beginning in 1922 to upgrade Mormon architecture. Designs of that period featured boldly stated architectural features, expressed here with the doorway and the quoins as well as the imposing front facade. Church construction from this period is rare in Nevada, so the preservation of this building is important to understand the architectural history of the region.

Later in the century, the Mormon Church constructed a new facility. Eventually, the White Pine Community Choir Association gained access to the 1927 building, which subsequently became a cultural center.

WESTSIDE SCHOOL

Like Caliente, Las Vegas prospered as a result of the railroad, its dependence on automobile traffic a thing of the future. The Las Vegas neighborhoods sprawled out from the community's core, and with that growth, the need for public education increased. The Westside School in Las Vegas was built in 1921 to address the needs of the increasing number of young people, a reality further answered by a large addition to the complex dating to 1948. The principal elevation of the original structure exhibits a simple Mission Revival entry with a parapet defined by curvilinear, sweeping lines. The building was otherwise simple in design. Whereas the original building had only two classrooms, a 1928 addition doubled that number. The later addition is a humble, low-lying brick-and-frame structure without any defining architectural style.

The Westside School was built in the "McWilliams Townsite," platted in 1904 in the northern part of the community. Minority and lower-income groups historically dominated the neighborhood, and the school consequently served Southern Paiutes and African Americans as they arrived in

The Las Vegas Westside School was built in 1921 for a minority and lower income neighborhood.

the neighborhood during the 1920s and 1930s. The Westside School is the oldest surviving institution of its type in the Las Vegas area, and is being transformed into a community center.

LAS VEGAS HIGH SCHOOL

Built in 1930, the Las Vegas High School was a response to southern Nevada prosperity during the early twentieth century. Some have described the remarkable expression of monumental Art Deco architecture as a rare example of Mayan Revival Art Deco architecture. In 1931, it was referred to as Aztec Moderne, and indeed, the school features some of the low, sweeping lines of the emerging Moderne style, but the design is more appropriately classified as Art Deco. Whatever the precise designation, the school exhibits a stunning approach to architecture. The reference to Central American culture derives from the images of two Native Americans, a man and a woman, who grace the ceremonial entrance to the school. The woman wears a cap that appears Peruvian.

The Reno architectural firm of George A. Ferris and Son designed the three-building complex, sited on Seventh Street in the heart of one of the oldest neighborhoods in Las Vegas. Securing the bonds needed for the construction met opposition both because the idea that five hundred students would attend seemed astounding and because the location seemed too far removed from town. Las Vegas quickly rose to the occasion as the community continued to grow, providing the students and demonstrating that it would, in fact, develop well beyond the area around the new high school.[10]

The Las Vegas High School has a full basement and two stories rising above ground level. The front elevation of the principal building includes three bays projecting before two recesses. The entire structure is marked by ground to roof buttresses. The main entrance includes a showcase of Art Deco bas-relief with vines entangling birds, fish, snakes, and other animals. The motif is repeated with vines and other designs in a decorative cast-concrete frieze forming a band at the roofline. The complex features the first monumental reinforced-concrete structure in the community.

This was the only high school in Las Vegas until the 1950s. At that time, the school district demolished one of the historic buildings, but the more significant main building with its elegant front facade survived. In addition, the name and purpose of the facility eventually changed. It is now the Las Vegas Academy of International Studies and Performing Arts, a districtwide magnet school with a mission to address the needs of students with specific academic and artistic interests. In spite of changes, the school remains a sentimental favorite for its thousands of alumni, regardless of the institution's name, as it nears the century mark of service to Nevada's youth.

HERITAGE HOUSE

What is now known as the Heritage House is one of many buildings displayed at the Clark County Museum in Henderson. Like the Las Vegas High School, this home reflects the early-twentieth-century emergence of wealth in southern Nevada. The building dates to 1931, a pivotal time of local development in the midst of the national economic depression. The firm of Warner and Norstrom designed the Tudor Revival house for Hakon "Jake" Hagenson, to be located on South Seventh Street near the Las Vegas High School. The house includes a steep gabled roof and exposed heavy timbers arranged in horizontal, vertical, and diagonal patterns and combined with plaster walls. Quaint wooden shutters and a porch balustrade, cobble-stone entrance, and chimney complete the traditional appearance of a building designed in keeping with the architecture of Tudor England.

Shortly after the home was constructed, Hagenson sold it to Pros J. Goumond, owner of the Boulder Club in Las Vegas. Goumond, who owned the house for a number of years, gave it a solid connection to the earliest period of the development of the Las Vegas casino industry. The Clark County Preservation Association obtained the house in 1981 and donated it to the Clark County Museum three years later. The structure sustained

FACING PAGE:

The 1930 Las Vegas High School is an elegant expression of Art Deco architecture. The facility is now known as the Las Vegas Academy of International Studies and Performing Arts.

In 1984, the Heritage House was moved to the Clark County Museum in Henderson. The 1931 Tudor Revival building was originally the home of Hakon "Jake" Hagenson.

some damage during the move, requiring extensive restoration, but the museum completed the task and the house now serves as an excellent venue to interpret Las Vegas history just as it was taking its first steps on the path to becoming an internationally famous tourist destination.

TAKEN TOGETHER, the buildings of the 1920s and early 1930s document Nevada as it was completing the transition from mining capital to tourism mecca. During this transformation, residents of the state conceived of new ways to exploit the range of opportunities. Nevadans once again cobbled together solutions using limited resources combined with ingenuity. The state's nineteenth-century architecture too often suffered because of the transient nature of its population. During the early twentieth century, the architecture often remained humble, but for a different reason. The first steps in the direction of tourism were modest, and the buildings reflect the limited financial resources available at that time. In spite of economic challenges, a new image of substance, permanence, and architectural style began to emerge in Nevada during those pivotal first decades of the century.

6 A New Deal

The era of the New Deal constitutes a distinct and exciting phase of Nevada's history. Responding to the challenges of the 1930s, the federal government worked with Nevadans to stimulate its economy. Key to this collaboration was the launching of construction projects across the state. The most famous of these projects was, of course, the taming of the mighty Colorado River with the construction of Hoover Dam. Envisioned during the 1920s before Roosevelt's New Deal, Hoover Dam became a reality during the decade of the 1930s, and once operating, it began to play a decisive role in southern Nevada development. An architectural marvel in its own right, the dam's presence and economic contribution spawned the construction of numerous other public and private buildings through-out Clark County, but the project ultimately affected the entire state.

Federal programs made substantial contributions to Nevada's cultural life, but their social and economic impact was even more significant. New Deal and other projects not only supplied jobs to unemployed Nevadans but also attracted thousands of other workers to the state, forever changing its demography and politics. Many of these immigrants chose to remain in Nevada even after New Deal projects ended. These people would contribute, therefore, to the state's dramatic social, economic, and demographic growth during the last decades of the twentieth century.

BOULDER CITY DEPOT

The Union Pacific Railroad Depot in Boulder City dates to 1931, a period when an enormous quantity of construction materials needed to be shipped to the area because of the Hoover Dam project. The depot was initially planned to handle only freight service, but accommodations for passengers later included a ticket office and an additional restroom. Within a year, passenger service proved unprofitable, and it was discontinued with the exception of special excursion trains.

Boulder City's Union Pacific Railroad Depot dates to 1931 when the Hoover Dam project was under way. The structure now resides at the Clark County Museum in Henderson.

Much of the appearance of the depot is typical of this building type. A hipped roof with wide overhangs is supported by exposed rafters and knee brackets. Horizontal clapboard siding clothes the structure. A freight platform stood ready to accept the large quantities of materials that would pass on the line. It is, however, a simple structure built for a specific and likely short-term purpose. The construction of the dam required many sorts of tools, and this depot fitted into this category. There was no reason to overbuild something that was intended to serve for only a few years. After the completion of Hoover Dam, use of the rail line predictably diminished, but World War II and the growth of Basic Magnesium, Inc., in Henderson increased activity on the Boulder branch of the Union Pacific. Use of the railroad was, nevertheless, temporary. In the mid-1970s, the Union Pacific Railroad abandoned the line past Henderson and donated the Boulder City depot to the Clark County Museum, where it was subsequently moved.[1]

BOULDER DAM HOTEL

In the wake of the economic growth associated with the construction of Hoover Dam, Boulder City emerged as a community destined to outlive the federal project. W. F. Grey and his wife, Virginia, were visiting Boulder City in the early 1930s when they realized the need for a hotel to capitalize on tourists who would be visiting the Dam. With a building permit in hand by 1932, the Greys hired Paul S. "Jim" Webb to construct the Boulder Dam Hotel. It opened the following year.[2]

The hotel was built in the Colonial Revival style of architecture in the heart of Boulder City. Its front elevation features a dramatic two-story porch with square paneled columns. The main entrance to the hotel lobby includes pilasters, quoins, and a pediment to add to the colonial feel of the design. The walls of the building are composed of small concrete blocks. In 1934, the Greys added a dining room and more hotel rooms. The following year, another wing provided even more rooms. The lobby represents the most significant interior space of the hotel. Paneling in southern

The Boulder Dam Hotel opened in 1933 in anticipation of tourists visiting Hoover Dam.

gumwood gives the room a warm, golden glow. At the far end of the room, a large brick fireplace surmounted by gumwood panels provides a decorative element seldom used in the heat of southern Nevada. A large wood-paneled staircase ascends to the rooms on the second floor.

In 1935, Webb went on to found Grand Canyon–Boulder Dam, Inc., a tourism agency, which purchased the hotel. Glover "Roxy" Ruckstell, inventor of the Ruckstell or Roxtell two-speed axle, provided much of the financial backing for Webb's acquisition. Ruckstell had recently arrived in Boulder City with his own tourism-related agenda that included airborne sightseeing tours of Hoover Dam and the Grand Canyon. Under the new management, the Boulder Dam Hotel prospered throughout the rest of the decade. Its elegant accommodations hosted presidents, royalty, and other international dignitaries.[3]

With the advent of World War II, increases in security restricted access to the dam and gas rationing reduced the number of people traveling to Boulder City. The hotel fell on hard times and never fully recovered. In the early 1990s, a nonprofit organization acquired the property, restored the building, and adapted it to serve as a museum. It rents rooms as a means to teach hotel management, in association with the University of Nevada System, and to raise revenue for the operation of the facility.

GRAND CANYON AIRLINES TICKET OFFICE

Yet another Boulder City structure became tied to the Boulder Dam Hotel and the effort to market the tourism potential of the region. The legislative session of 1931 was pivotal for the state. In an effort to inoculate Nevada from the effects of the Great Depression, legislators legalized gambling and shortened the period of residency needed for a divorce. The state took the first small steps toward making itself one of the great tourist draws of the nation. Visitors had been attracted to the area for decades because of the area's natural beauty, but the lure of gambling and easy divorces made the state even more attractive for many.[4]

Shortly after the legislature took such a radical approach to sin and tourism, Grand Canyon Airlines opened a ticket office at Bullock Field,

A primitive office in Boulder City served the Grand Canyon Airlines in the 1930s. It is now on exhibit at the Clark County Museum in Henderson.

the Boulder City airport at the time.[5] This was the first substantial sight-seeing airline business in the area. Glover Ruckstell, who had invested in the purchase of the Boulder Dam Hotel, operated the business, which gave people the opportunity to see Hoover Dam and the Grand Canyon from a bird's-eye view. By the mid-1930s, Ruckstell moved the building to a resi-dential neighborhood in the community to house Henry and Ocie Bradley, the first African American family allowed to live in Boulder City. The Bradleys worked for Ruckstell, Henry as a bartender and general assistant, with Ocie making sandwiches for the Grand Canyon Airlines.

By 1936, Ruckstell's business became part of the larger effort known as Grand Canyon–Boulder Dam Tours, which had recently acquired the Boulder Dam Hotel. The corporation earned the first concessionaire relationship with the National Park Service to fly over the future Lake Mead National Recreation Area. When the original ticket office–turned-home partially burned in 1939, the Bradleys moved to a new house on the outskirts of Boulder City. The original structure was repaired and subse-quently served a succession of owners and residents.[6]

The building was an extremely simple clapboard-sided structure, with a long gable roof spanning the length of its elongated rectangular form. The front third of the building was an open porch protected by the roof and framed by partial walls. Eventually, this part of the building was enclosed to increase the habitable space.

The building has considerable significance given its association with an early experiment in the state's tourism industry. The fact that it also housed the first African Americans living in Boulder City adds to its importance. By the end of the twentieth century, the future of the under-stated building was uncertain. The property owner offered it to the Clark County Museum in Henderson in 2001, where it subsequently moved.

LOS ANGELES WATER AND POWER BUILDING

Constructed in 1940, Boulder City's Los Angeles Water and Power Build-ing was an administrative center for the regulation of power and water on the lower Colorado River. The structure was an additional example of the nation's enormous program associated with Hoover Dam and the effort to harness the power of the Colorado for public use. Los Angeles Water and Power, one of the beneficiaries of the dam, needed a facility in southern Nevada, and so the agency constructed this structure for that purpose.

The building exhibits eclectic motifs, causing people to refer to it as both American and Spanish Colonial Revival style. The overall massing of the structure has nothing to do with any sort of colonial revival, and, ultimately, the design should be regarded as vernacular. The facility features space for offices but also a large auditorium for use as a community center. The irregular shape of the building includes a multisided tower for the main entrance and an interior courtyard. The one-story building is made with concrete block with extruded mortar to provide texture. A hip roof covers most of the structure except for the shops, where there is a shed roof.

The 1940 Los Angeles Water and Power Building in Boulder City provided a facility for the Southern California agency as it managed its interest in Hoover Dam's output.

Inside, walls include a low wainscoting completed in tile with a colorful arabesque motif. The ceiling of the auditorium is composed of redwood joists and sheathing. The tile floor of the foyer includes an emblem for Los Angeles Water and Power. In 1995, the agency transferred ownership of its facility to Boulder City, which has worked to place the structure into service as a multipurpose community and cultural center.

LAS VEGAS FEDERAL COURTHOUSE AND POST OFFICE

The Las Vegas Federal Courthouse and Post Office is one of the most important historic resources in the state. Constructed between 1931 and 1933, the building was yet another response to the growth inspired by the Hoover Dam project. In addition, it was built in the wake of legalized gambling and a shortened period of residency for divorce, both of which had

enhanced the Nevada economy in the midst of decline elsewhere during the Great Depression.

The Las Vegas federal building was an imposing presence in Las Vegas, long before the community grew into the giant that would dominate the postwar state. The Neoclassical design of the building is typical of period U.S. Treasury Department projects. The building is three stories, with a raised first floor over a basement. For dramatic effect and to enhance the dignity of the federal presence, a broad staircase ascends to seven round-arched openings with windows and doors. Above that, ascending from the second to third floors, are eight pilasters with Ionic capitals separating banks of large windows for each floor. The first floor, the pilasters, and a classical parapet with railing are completed in terra-cotta. The walls of the upper floors are finished in yellow brick.

The first floor of the building was dedicated to postal work and included a lobby with post office boxes, counters for service to the public, and a large area for sorting mail. The upper floors were mostly used for office space to accommodate federal agencies and for the federal court, which included a large courtroom. Much of the interior is finished in hardwoods with molded plaster featuring eagles, pilasters, and various other details.

The Las Vegas Post Office has local significance as an expression of the federal presence in southern Nevada and because of its monumental architecture constructed at a time when this sort of building effort was relatively rare in the community. The post office and courthouse acquired national importance as one of the more notable meeting locations of the U.S. Senate Special Committee to Investigate Organized Crime in Interstate Commerce, commonly called the "Kefauver Committee," after its chairman, Estes Kefauver (1903–1963). The seventh of its fourteen hearings occurred in this Las Vegas facility. Because of the growth of the gaming industry in Las Vegas and its notorious connections with the Mafia, the

FACING PAGE:

The Las Vegas Federal Courthouse and Post Office was an early monumental presence in Las Vegas, dating to the 1930s. The City of Las Vegas, which manages the property, is restoring it to serve as a museum.

hearing in southern Nevada had special significance. On a statewide level, the hearing can be regarded as playing a pivotal role in setting the stage for reforms that led to the creation of the Nevada Gaming Commission.

Kefauver used the fame he gained at the helm of the committee to launch bids for the presidency in 1952 and 1956. He was the vice presidential nominee on the Democratic ticket in 1956, running with Adlai Stevenson. Although all of these election bids failed, Kefauver had gained stature with his distinguished career and especially because of his work on his committee. Ironically, the committee hearings helped the gaming industry in Nevada. By focusing on the relationship of the Mob to gambling, other states clamped down on the activity, leaving Nevada with something of a monopoly. In addition, it gave the state's industry national publicity. With tightening state controls emerging, the public had less concern that Nevada's casinos were "rigged," and a common penchant to rub shoulders with the illicit could consequently be sated with a relatively tame visit to Las Vegas.

HAWTHORNE SIXTH STREET SCHOOL

Nevada is famed for its link to the gaming industry, and Hoover Dam wins the area its own form of recognition, but another factor important to the growth of the state in the twentieth century was the U.S. military. Hawthorne, as discussed in chapter 2, is a town like none other in the state. Although its roots are typical enough, its subsequent development was linked to a federal interest in developing a national arms depot. Founded in 1881 as a terminus of the Carson and Colorado Railway to take advantage of the region's mineral potential, Hawthorne enjoyed some success as a mercantile center in southwestern Nevada, and it became the seat for Esmeralda County in 1883. The strange twist in Hawthorne's local economy and character occurred when the United States Naval Ammunition Depot opened in 1929. This occurred three years after the accidental detonation in New Jersey of approximately one million pounds of ordinance at one of the navy's principal depots. Hawthorne quickly became the nation's largest repository for explosives and other weaponry, and it played a critical role in the distribution of war matériel during the Second World War.

The ammunition depot gave Hawthorne a thriving economy and a degree of longevity it would not have enjoyed by depending solely on the mining industry. Because the depot remained a consistent employer in town, construction of new buildings was possible even in the midst of the Great Depression. In 1936, the Mineral County School District sold its fifty-year-old school for $2.10 so a salvage crew could scavenge the lumber and clear the lot, making way for a modern facility. Funding for the replacement came from the New Deal Public Works Administration.

Architect Willis H. Church designed the new Sixth Street School in a subtle adaptation of the Art Deco style, popular at the time. The low one-story building featured four classrooms and a basement with restrooms and storage. Two subsequent additions provided more rooms and an auditorium until the complex included ten thousand square feet on the

Hawthorne built its Sixth Street School with federal funds from the Public Works Administration, a New Deal program in the 1930s. After 1997, the facility became an arts center.

main level and fifteen hundred square feet in the basement. The two front doors are framed by shallow projecting bays, and the exterior is treated in stucco. Simple pilasters flank the doors and reach toward parapets.

Hawthorne's Sixth Street School closed in the 1980s and subsequently served as a storage area for the school district. In 1997, the Mineral County Council on the Arts assumed control of the school and transformed the building into a cultural center, using its auditorium as a theater.

CITY OF RENO SOUTHSIDE SCHOOL ANNEX

Reno's annex to its Southside School also dates to 1936 and is similarly a New Deal adaptation of the Art Deco style of design. Today, the two-story brick building dominates the adjacent parking lot, balancing a low-lying structure that formerly served as the Reno City Hall on the southeast side of the block. The Southside School was built in the corner of a lot that originally featured, at its center, an older school built in 1903. The turn-of-the-century building was demolished in 1960 to make way for the new municipal facility.

The 1936 school annex is an unusual collection of architectural motifs. The entrance dominates an oddly proportioned angular tower. The doorway is framed in cast concrete, surmounted by an angular motif that rises to a second-story window, itself capped by whimsical plants and an owl also formed in concrete. The tower is balanced by a similar structure at the rear, although this one is composed without detail. The rest of the school features rather conventional classical elements, including quoins shaped by raised and recessed brick and pedimented gables with eave returns. A seven-sided one-story tower protrudes from the side, echoing the front and back entrances. Inside, a fireplace is framed with tiles fired with bas-relief images from the Old King Cole nursery rhyme.

The City of Reno purchased the Southside School from the school district in 1959, but the building continued to serve for many years as a community recreation center for students. A restoration effort begun in 2006 transformed the school into a cultural center serving diverse interests and constituents.

Reno's 1936 Southside School once served students on the south side of the river. It is now a cultural center for the inner city.

FIRST CHURCH OF CHRIST, SCIENTIST

Reno's First Church of Christ, Scientist is another example of grand architecture undertaken in Reno in the 1930s. The building is a monumental Nevada example of work by the prestigious Southern California architect Paul Revere Williams. Known as "the architect to the stars," Williams was the first African American member of the American Institute of Architects. During his remarkable career, Williams designed hundreds of buildings, including several in Nevada. His southern Nevada clients included such notables as Lucille Ball and Desi Arnaz, Lon Chaney, Tyrone Power, Martin Landau, William "Bojangles" Robinson, and Walter Winchell.[7]

Although Williams demonstrated mastery of many styles, including those of the avant-garde, his church in Reno was a staid expression of the Neoclassical Revival style, by then in use for many years. The two-story structure dates to 1939 and stands on the north side of the Truckee River, several blocks to the west of the downtown commercial corridor.

A pair of curving staircases leads up to a terrace and portico with four

Prominent African American architect Paul Revere Williams from California designed Reno's First Church of Christ, Scientist in the 1930s. In 1998, the Reno-Sparks Theater Coalition acquired the property with the help of Moya Lear, widow of Bill Lear, inventor and aviation pioneer.

slender two-story columns for a dramatic entrance into the building. The portico is capped with a pediment, decorated with a sunburst fanlight extended by radiating molding that fills the entire gable end with the motif. A dentil cornice adds to the classical air of the church, as do the three front doors, the center of which is crowned with a decorative pediment, echoing the larger feature about the portico. A pair of one-over-one windows with decorative grills adorns either side of the doors of the front facade, providing further balanced symmetry. The interior of the church consists of a spacious auditorium with a small balcony to the rear.

In 1998, the congregation sold their building to the Reno-Sparks Theater Coalition. Moya Lear, widow of Bill Lear, famed inventor and aviation developer, made a substantial donation to the institution to facilitate the purchase of the property, earning the honor of lending her name to the facility, subsequently known as the Lear Theater. The organization replaced a small stage with a larger one to accommodate performances and pursued the rehabilitation of the building, but work remains unfinished and the fate of the theater is uncertain.

STEWART INDIAN SCHOOL

The Stewart Indian School, founded in 1890 south of Carson City, is another example of development in northern Nevada during the 1920s and 1930s. The founding of the institution represents a sometimes tragic nineteenth-century federal experiment in the interaction with Native Americans. The school is a rare survivor of a program implemented by the Bureau of Indian Affairs beginning in the latter part of the 1800s. The philosophy behind the program stressed assimilation, beginning with the younger generation. The schools were intended to provide education removed from the reservation, controlling the environment so children would be forced to adopt the English language and Euro-American culture. The federal government established twenty-five of these schools,

Stewart Indian School, to the south of Carson City, was one of a few off-reservation federal schools built for Native Americans. The campus includes dozens of historic buildings, most of which were built by students learning how to become masons.

but Stewart was the only one to operate in Nevada. It survives as one of the best preserved in the nation. The school takes its name from Nevada U.S. senator William Stewart.[8]

At the opening of the school, Paiute, Washoe, and Shoshone children were forcibly taken from their families. Stories recount how parents came to Stewart so they could camp beyond the fence with the hope of having some contact with their children. The tragic chapter added to ill will inspired by the Euro-Americans' taking of Native American resources and land during the nineteenth century. More than one hundred children represented the initial student body.

As a cornerstone of assimilation, Stewart students received vocational training so they could acquire jobs upon graduation. Boys were educated in agriculture and the building trades, while girls received training in the domestic arts. The school included acreage devoted to crops, in part to provide an education in agriculture but also to raise food consumed by the students. In spite of the disagreeable aspects of the school, some Native Americans sought an education for their children, believing it was their best hope for successful survival in the new era. In addition, the first superintendent of the school, W. D. C. Gibson, quickly relaxed many of the harsher aspects of the federal program, repeatedly making choices that increased the attractiveness of the school to Native Americans.

In 1894, when the first graduates found inadequate employment opportunities, those still enrolled threatened to abandon the school, but Stewart's doors remained open, and its best days were ahead. In 1896, Gibson provided discarded musical instruments in ill repair to the students, and the school marching band became an instant success. Students were particularly attracted to the drums, and late-night practice sessions became the means to hold forbidden Native dances. Gibson chose to look the other way because it was good for morale. When the Stewart Marching Band took first place in the 1897 Nevada Day Parade, applications for school enrollment increased by several hundred.

Throughout the early period of Stewart's history, its buildings proved inadequate. After the 1919 arrival of a new superintendent, Frederick Snyder, the institution addressed this gap. Beginning in 1923, Snyder instituted a program of adding to Stewart's building stock with stone structures, designed to last. The superintendent began training boys in masonry, and they earned practical experience erecting a large number of the school buildings. The majority of the roughly eighty historic structures surviving at Stewart are the product of the efforts of Snyder and his students.

Snyder's buildings have a distinct, unmistakable appearance. The superintendent preferred the look of multicolored untrimmed stones laid in random courses. He was known to scour the desert in search of suitable rock. Black mortar, produced by adding charcoal, accented rhyolite and other rocks with their shades of pink, green, and brown. Most of Snyder's structures are one story with gables and shake or metal roofs. Some include a second story, and many have porches. Coursed stone typically outlines windows and doors. The design of these buildings was heavily influenced by the Arts and Crafts movement, and many look like bungalows. Others exhibit classical influences, but the dominant theme is the random coursed, colorful rock. These buildings became the hallmark of the school, a means for training students, and an often used option in the region's architecture.

By the mid-twentieth century, Carson City had sprawled south and embraced the Stewart campus, which nevertheless retained its separate identity and character. The school had become such a popular institution among Native Americans that students from as far away as Arizona were in attendance. Its basketball team, wrestlers, and school band gained widespread respect for remarkable performances, and Stewart became a matter of profound pride among Native Americans.

In 1981, Secretary of the Interior James Watt, seeking to remove the federal government from the role of running schools, declared the structures at Stewart to be seismically unstable, even though there was no solid evidence that this was the case. The school closed, and most of the campus was eventually transferred to the State of Nevada, with the understanding that at least one of the buildings would be used by the Native American community to interpret the history of Stewart and the various tribes living in Nevada. The Nevada Indian Commission operates an interpretive center at Stewart, and the state is restoring and occupying an increasing number of buildings, contributing to a vibrant campus.[9]

THUNDERBIRD LODGE

Because Stewart graduates became masons in the community, their legacy extends far beyond the boundaries of the school. The importance of their work is underscored by the fact that two non-Stewart buildings discussed in this book were erected by these craftsmen. Snyder's program and his graduates have come to represent one of the most important local contributions to northern Nevada's architectural history. As Native Americans received training, they could not imagine they would be employed by one of the more eccentric millionaires on the West Coast.

In 1936, George Whittell Jr., sole heir to two enormous Gold Rush–era fortunes, purchased twenty-seven miles of Lake Tahoe shoreline. Consisting of nearly all of the Nevada part of the basin, the holdings extended to the eastern crest of the Sierra Nevada, and in some cases even beyond that point. Born in 1881, Whittell loved fast boats, cars, and planes. And women were high on his list as well. When World War I began, he could not resist the call of adventure, and so he volunteered as an ambulance driver on the Italian front. With the entry of the United States into the conflict, he became a captain in the army, a commission his father purchased on his son's behalf.

Whittell was committed to not working, but he made one astute business move that made all the rest possible: he sold his entire stock portfolio in the summer of 1929, missing the crash by a few months. With fifty million dollars in cash and enormous San Francisco real estate holdings, Whittell had the power to do anything he wished, even in the midst of the Great Depression. A connoisseur of Deusenbergs and wild animals,

The Whittell Mansion, often called the Thunderbird Lodge, occupies one of the most beautiful sites in the West. Frederic DeLongchamps designed the complex, which was built in part by Native American masons trained at the Stewart Indian School.

he owned six of the precious automobiles and kept elephants, cheetahs, giraffes, zebras, and lions, including his favorite, "Bill," at his Bay Area estate.

In 1936, Norman Biltz, a real estate developer in Nevada, offered Whittell the opportunity to purchase the holdings of four Comstock-era lumber companies whose land was worth little undeveloped but required the payment of taxes to maintain ownership. The move allowed the multimillionaire to dream of grandiose developments of lakeshore casinos, but he never followed through; to do so would have been too much like work. Instead, he settled for the construction of one of Tahoe's greatest private estates.

Beginning in 1936, Whittell collaborated with Nevada's premier architect, Frederic DeLongchamps, who initially proposed a low-lying mountain log cabin designed to blend into the hills surrounding Sand Harbor. Whittell rejected the proposal, even though it was probably a response to what he had requested: DeLongchamps was an expert at giving his clients exactly what they wanted, and his designs were rarely rejected. After many drafts and changes, DeLongchamps arrived at the final plan for a complex that consisted of a main lodge, a tunnel connecting it to a boathouse, a garage combined with an elephant house, and numerous other structures providing space for servants and other purposes.

Between 1938 and 1940, a diverse ensemble of workers constructed one of Nevada's most striking historic sites. Stonemasons, including many Native Americans who had graduated from Stewart Indian School, crafted the walls of the buildings. They also created a three-story waterfall and meandering, whimsical paths that connect the acreage and the structures, turning a majestic, beautiful setting into a place of unparalleled magic. Norwegian carpenters completed the interior work and constructed rafters and vaulted ceilings for the steeply pitched roofs. Their distinctive brand of woodwork is visible throughout the buildings.

Italian ironworkers crafted forest scenes of trees and squirrels and other animals to decorate the towering stone chimneys that accent both sides of each of the structures. The immigrants also forged outdoor lanterns, andirons, and screens for the dozens of fireplaces, and many other objects decorating the compound. Finally, DeLongchamps, himself always devoted to the mining industry, employed Cornish miners from the Comstock to excavate hundreds of feet of tunnel through solid granite. As much as three stories below ground, the tunnels provide access to a furnace room, the first boathouse, a larger boathouse, and a lake-level portal to bring in supplies. Stonemasons used the shattered debris from the tunnel work to add to the landscaping. Many of these rocks exhibit the blown-away halves of drill holes, which one normally finds around historic mine sites.

With random coursed stone, steeply pitched roofs, and quaint architectural details, the complex can be regarded as English Cottage Revival. Several decades before, in Reno, DeLongchamps designed a similar structure—often called his honeymoon cottage—but it was much smaller. The Whittell property exhibits this style on a grand scale. Hidden by the forest and hills from the highway, the property has been a curiosity for decades for boaters. Even so, the true magnificence of the resource can be appreciated only by walking along the paths or looking at the lake from one of the windows inside the comfortable lodge.

Whittell visited his "castle," as he called it, during summer months throughout the rest of his life. He died in 1969, leaving enough money to support his widow, but giving most of his estate to organizations for the conservation of animals and habitats. He had imagined commercial development of his Lake Tahoe property, but ultimately his sloth won out and his legacy is thousands of acres of pristine alpine forest. International investor Jack Dreyfus purchased thousands of acres including the lodge from the Whittell estate. The complex was subsequently acquired as part of a land exchange with the U.S. Forest Service. The actual buildings are managed by the Thunderbird Lodge Preservation Association, which hosts tours and special events, inviting the public to glimpse the consequences of incredible wealth in the midst of national depression.[10]

WUNGNEMA HOUSE

Carson City's Wungnema House is another fine example of the work of Stewart graduates. Finished after World War II, the home actually employed a style of construction different from that of the Stewart Indian School. Native American masons used stone as a veneer over a wood frame for the house, unlike the solid stone walls at the school. Nevertheless, the effect has the same appearance. Burton and Pearl Wungnema built the house and raised eight children there. They were members of the Hopi Tribe and, together with their parents, had come from Arizona, in part to attend the Stewart Indian School.[11]

The two-story home includes dormers and roof gables finished in wooden shingles. A large chimney dominates one of the sides, and a porch greets visitors on another. Windows have concrete sills and heads. The

Burton and Pearl Wungnema, of the Hopi Water Clan, came to Carson City because of the Stewart Indian School. They built their home in the late 1940s and operated a quarry until the death of Burton Wungnema in 1956

interior stone fireplace bears lightning and clouds crafted from stone, emblems of the Hopi Water Clan to which the Wungnemas belonged. Rather than using the multicolored rock typical of the Stewart complex, the Wungnemas used only rose-colored rhyolite for their house, quarried from Burton Wungnema's father's quarry in Brunswick Canyon, east of Carson City.

Burton Wungnema died in 1956, and his widow and family moved to a larger house in the 1970s to accommodate a growing number of grand-children. By then, sprawling Carson City had surrounded the house, situated near the eastern border of Mills Park. A developer acquired the house, hoping to use it for a restaurant, but plans failed to materialize and Carson City subsequently purchased the home and added its acreage to the park. The house now serves as the location for a wide variety of events held in the park.[12]

CARSON CITY CIVIC AUDITORIUM

Another example of impressive 1930s architecture in Carson City owes its support to federal New Deal funding. Nevada architect Lehman A. Ferris designed a civic auditorium for Carson City in 1938. Herb Louis Dressler constructed the building the following year, with support from the Public Works Administration. The auditorium was sited on the location of the former National Guard Armory, later used by the American Legion as a fraternal hall. It burned down in the mid-1930s, clearing the lot and creating the need for a new community hall. The subsequent civic auditorium opened in 1939.

The single-story brick structure stands on an elevated basement, giving it an imposing presence on the main street, with a large staircase leading up to the twin front doors. Trimmed in cream-colored concrete that contrasts against the red brick, the doors are flanked and separated by Ionic pilasters, supporting a large half-circle fanlight window. Echoing this theme, multipaned windows appear in pairs, divided by an Ionic pilaster and capped with a simple rounded arch made of brick. Decorative brick, laid in a saw-toothed pattern and descending into rakes with a repetitive series of rounded arches, dominates the front gable. The net effect of the design refers to the Romanesque Revival movement, which had been passé for several decades by the time of the construction of the civic auditorium, but the style nevertheless continued to resonate in public buildings.

The front of the structure opens onto a lobby area, separate from the expansive hall. Inside is the auditorium, which dominates the interior. The large meeting space has a hardwood floor and raised stage at the far end. A full basement provides additional space for meetings and offices.

For roughly a dozen years after the building's opening, various groups used the facility, but occupancy steadily declined by the mid-1950s. At that point, the newly created county library and various other government offices took over space in the building. Eventually, they relocated, leaving the auditorium largely abandoned in 1983. In early 1990, the Children's Museum of Northern Nevada assumed management of the historic structure.

OVERTON GYMNASIUM

At the same time that Carson City was using New Deal funding to build its civic auditorium, Miles Miller of Salt Lake City designed the gymnasium for Overton at the southern end of the state in 1938. The community was one of several founded over the decades by attempts—often led by Mormon settlers from Utah—to farm the well-watered land along the Muddy and Virgin rivers to the north and northeast of Las Vegas. During the 1860s, members of the Church of Jesus Christ of Latter-day Saints established two missions—St. Thomas and St. Joseph—along the Muddy River, with the goal of raising cotton for the Mormon textile industry. Despite the area's intense heat, the settlements survived, but the communities largely disbanded when it became clear that the area was part of Nevada and state officials demanded back taxes. Many church members left, but eventually others returned and rebuilt some of the abandoned homes, reworked the fields, and established new settlements in the valley. The resettlement of the Muddy River valley proved a success, and over the decades, several permanent communities grew up along the shores of the Muddy.

Miller provided plans for the Overton Gymnasium funded by the federal Public Works Administration. The structure was subsequently surrounded by a later school building, but the architect's original edifice retains a high degree of integrity. The gym is composed of faux bricks made of tinted concrete. Windows were originally capped with rounded arches, which were subsequently covered. Terra-cotta details include fluted classical columns on either side of the doorway, itself surmounted by a rounded-arch fanlight, with an exaggerated keystone. The entryway also has portholes, a motif used throughout the exterior, and a full terra-cotta entablature defines the first and second stories in the front elevation and around the sides. Lesser terra-cotta keystones are repeated in the redbrick arches above windows throughout the building. The tops of buttresses supporting the sidewalls are also accented with terra-cotta.

FACING PAGE:
Lehman Ferris designed Carson City's Civic Auditorium in 1938. The federal Public Works Administration paid for its construction.

The school gymnasium in Overton dates to the late 1930s, yet another facility funded by the New Deal.

The building can be regarded as Italian Renaissance Revival. It is unusual for the use of terra-cotta, a rarity in southern Nevada, and for the application of red-colored concrete bricks. After the turn of the millennium, a nonprofit organization opened the old gym as a cultural center.

LOGANDALE ELEMENTARY SCHOOL

Logandale is another example of a place heavily influenced by the attempts of Mormon settlements to develop the Muddy and Virgin rivers. The town was founded a few miles upstream from Overton and took its name from the Logans, a prominent family of early settlers. By 1933, Logandale claimed some three hundred residents, and as the southern Nevada population grew in the wake of the Hoover Dam projects, its prospects improved. In 1935, the residents of Logandale consolidated the community's various elementary schools, housed in small wooden structures, into a single facility. That year, local volunteers quarried limestone and built their new school, which was enlarged the following year. Before the end of the decade, the Public Works Administration funded the addition of a substantial brick facade to the new educational building. Miles Miller, the Salt Lake City architect who also designed the Overton Gymnasium, provided the plans for this addition. Although the building grew out of a

The Logandale Elementary School dates to 1935 but was modified with additions twice before the end of the decade.

haphazard series of construction periods, there was a clear effort to create a substantial, monumental presence in the community.[13]

The first phase of construction for the Logandale Elementary School follows a plan that has been called "Starved Classicism." That is to say, it has Neoclassical lines but is lacking some of the details normally associated with the style. In 1936, a stone addition added more classrooms on the north elevation. This has a Mission Revival curvilinear parapet and an exquisite use of stone to define the rounded arch of the doorway. Miller's substantial addition dating to 1938 includes Spanish Colonial Revival elements, as it switched the main entrance to the east elevation. A large auditorium with a stage dominates the center of the facility.

The Logandale school closed in 1976, but it continued to serve as a community center and as the local court facility for the justice of the peace until 1995. Deferred maintenance resulted in the need for extensive repairs, and the possibility of demolition loomed. In 1997, a restoration project commenced with the establishment of the Old Logandale School Historic and Cultural Society.[14]

MESQUITE OLD GYMNASIUM

Miles Miller, the architect in Salt Lake City who had designed Overton Gymnasium and the front facade of the Logandale Elementary School, also provided plans for the gymnasium in Mesquite, another community that was part of the river settlements north of Las Vegas. Miller's Mesquite building dates to 1939, the year after his work in Overton. The Public Works Administration funded the facility in Mesquite, following a pattern familiar with Miller's other southern Nevada projects. The facility was completed by Salzner-Thompson, contractors.[15]

Four substantial fluted pilasters mark the ceremonial entrance to the building, and a sizable cornice with entablature demarcates the roofline. As with Miller's other southern Nevada work, a rounded arch surmounts the main doorway. He also repeated the unusual use, found in Overton, of red-tinted concrete faux brick and terra-cotta details. Banks of east-facing windows were designed to give access to ample light in the early mornings. The structure is a more sedate version of the Overton Gymnasium, but it clearly makes the same architectural references and can be regarded as influenced by the Italian Renaissance Revival.

By the early 1990s, the facility had become home to the Virgin Valley Medical Clinic, the local justice court, and the Mesquite Senior Center. After a turn-of-the-century restoration, it reopened as a cultural center.

MESQUITE DESERT VALLEY MUSEUM AND LIBRARY

Another structure in Mesquite attracted the public's attention, justifying preservation into the next century. The home of the Mesquite Desert Valley Museum and Library dates to 1941, a rare example of a public building funded by the National Youth Administration (NYA). The New Deal program was intended as a counterbalance to the Civilian Conservation Corps (CCC), a means to employ America's unemployed youth who no longer attended school. The CCC occasionally inspired young people to drop out of school in order to enjoy the benefits of employment. The NYA was intended to provide work for students who remained in school, in an

TOP: Mesquite's school gymnasium dates to 1939. Salt Lake City architect Miles Miller provided the plans.

BOTTOM: The 1941 Mesquite Desert Valley Museum and Library is a rare example of a building associated with the National Youth Administration. Its Pueblo Revival architecture is equally uncommon in Nevada.

effort to encourage the continued pursuit of education. NYA funding, which usually supported on-campus work, was only rarely used for construction. Nevada has two examples of building projects supported by this program: a vocational education building in Lovelock and a small museum and library in Mesquite. In both cases, the work was intended to give students vocational training in construction.[16]

The Mesquite structure is a rare expression of Pueblo Revival architecture, a style most notably employed in the nearby Lost City Museum, also a Depression-era project. Mesquite's structure is a humble use of noncoursed stone with a flat roof featuring ridgepoles. Other elements associated with Pueblo-style construction include the low massing of the building, the dual doors, the protruding drain spouts, and the projecting pine poles to support the flat roof. During the course of construction, funding ran out when the walls had reached the top of the windows. Volunteers provided the supplies and labor needed to finish the project. The walls bear the imprint of this transition: the lower level is made up of smaller stones, whereas time-saving larger blocks were used for the upper courses.

The facility housed the local museum and library for about a year before becoming a local health clinic and hospital. In 1977, it was abandoned, but in 1985, the Boy Scouts took it over and turned it into the Desert Valley Museum. A restoration in 1999 addressed structural problems that had evolved over the decades, giving the building the opportunity to serve as a museum well into the following century.

NEVADANS combined New Deal programs with their own innovative approaches to improve the economy with legalized gambling and liberalized divorce laws. The effect was to make development dollars more plentiful than they were in many other places. The population was still limited, but those who lived in the state were able to make substantial contributions to the architectural heritage of Nevada.

7 Inventing the Future

The meaning of the term *historic* shifts with time. Eventually, modern buildings grow older and, if they survive, are recognized as historic. Futuristic structures of the late 1950s and 1960s were designed with little regard to history, so it is with a bit of irony that they can now be regarded as significant expressions of the past. One of the problems with interpreting and preserving resources from this period is that their importance is not yet universally accepted or understood. Buildings experience a transformation at some point, often when they deteriorate and owners begin to consider discarding them in favor of modern development. If people recognize the significance of a building before it is demolished or falls down, then the resource stands a chance to survive. The fact that most buildings do not survive while passing through this bottleneck is what makes those with a historic designation revered. Buildings discussed in this chapter are in the bottleneck. It remains to be seen which ones will survive so their importance will be understood by enough of the community to become widely respected and preserved.

The social and economic prosperity Nevada experienced during the last half of the twentieth century encouraged cultural innovation. Tourism had played an important role in the state's economic life since the late 1920s. As the nation grew more prosperous over the course of the twentieth century and as its labor force acquired longer periods of leisure time, Nevada became a popular tourist destination. Having learned through the decades how best to accommodate the entertainment needs and desires of its guests, the state emerged as an international leader and a cultural innovator in the field of tourism.

Nevada's groundbreaking spirit during this era was reflected in its buildings. Beginning in the 1940s and continuing into the twenty-first century, the state's modern, ultramodern, and postmodern architecture has inspired the nation's cutting-edge designers and won a unique place for the state in the history of design. Six structures illustrate some of the possibilities during the state's development in the last half of the twentieth century.

HUNTRIDGE THEATER

The opening of the Huntridge Theater in 1944 was a welcomed event in Las Vegas, providing as it did an opportunity to see the latest Hollywood had to offer. The theater also represented an imposing expression of modern architecture. In retrospect, the Huntridge Theater is more conventional and conservative than contemporaries might have thought at first, but it was, nevertheless, an architectural step into the modern.[1]

Built as the community's only nonsegregated theater, the Huntridge was designed as a streamlined Moderne statement, a style that seemed to rush into the future. S. Charles Lee, a theater architect with a national reputation, designed the building. A seventy-five-foot fluted tower accented with a large round opening and capped with the name of the theater in neon lights distinguishes what is otherwise an unremarkable exterior. The one-story brick and concrete building has a shallow bowed roof. With the exception of the tower, much of its appearance, both outside and inside, is understated. The only windows are associated with the simple entrance to the lobby, where molded patterns in the ceiling offer some of the few distinct interior elements.

The Moderne-style Huntridge Theater in Las Vegas dates to 1944.

By the late 1970s, the theater had fallen on hard times, faced with competition from modern multiplexes. In 1992, the Friends of the Huntridge Theater, a nonprofit organization, obtained the property. In 1995, the weight of air-conditioning units combined with rotting support timbers caused the roof to collapse. In spite of the setback, dogged dedication restored the facility, and it reopened better than ever.

The Huntridge thrived as a concert venue and movie theater for nearly a decade, annually welcoming about seventy-five thousand young people, many of them minorities or economically disadvantaged. It hosted such diverse cultural events as SPIKE & MIKE's Animation Festival, the CINEVEGAS Film Festival, Mexican Comedy, children's theater, and dance concerts. Declining revenue forced the theater to close in 2001, and the nonprofit organization sold the property to settle its mortgage. Ever since then, the Huntridge has remained vacant and subject to vandalism. A venue that was a fine movie house and then a hip concert hall waits for a third incarnation that will prevent its demolition in a community known for the way it discards remnants of the past.

MOULIN ROUGE

The vulnerability of historic resources is nowhere more apparent than with the Moulin Rouge, situated near the border between Las Vegas and North Las Vegas. The Moulin Rouge opened as a hotel casino on May 24, 1955. It was constructed on the edge of the Westside, a predominately African American neighborhood.

The Moulin Rouge was the first nonsegregated establishment of its kind in the region. Open for only a matter of months, the hotel-casino nevertheless provided a venue where African American entertainers could perform in a relaxed environment in front of interracial audiences. Singers and groups such as Stump and Stumpy, the Bill Johnson Quartette, Wild Bill Davis, the Ahmad Jamal Trio, the Platters, Maurice and Gregory Hines, Lionel Hampton, and Dinah Washington performed there. Others such as Frank Sinatra, Dean Martin, Harry Belafonte, Louis Armstrong, Tallulah Bankhead, Sammy Davis Jr., Lena Horne, Pearl Bailey, and Nat "King" Cole went to the Moulin Rouge after appearing at larger all-white casinos to the south on the Strip, and occasionally they participated in impromptu performances or jam sessions. Former heavyweight boxing champion Joe Louis was the official host for the business.

Like the Huntridge, a towering sign dominated the exterior of the hotel-casino. The name "Moulin Rouge," a reference to the famous Parisian institution of the "red windmill," is featured in neon lights in the shape of cursive writing at the top of the four-story tower. Las Vegas

The Moulin Rouge opened in 1955. It represented an important benchmark in the integration of Nevada hotel casinos.

architects Walter Zick and Harris Sharp designed the complex, which included a one-story casino and theater and a V-shaped two-story hotel. The casino was covered in stucco and featured projecting square pavilions and a shingled mansard roof. The hotel had a shallow gable roof and modest appointments. Within the courtyard enclosed by the casino and hotel was a concrete pool.

The large casino included a long wooden bar and a small raised platform that could serve as a stage, although a larger theater occupied a separate space to the rear of the building. The walls of the casino were decorated with lively, colorful murals illustrating African American can-can dancers, well-appointed cars, and fancily dressed onlookers. The theater had a stepped purple stucco ceiling that complemented the excellent acoustics of the room.

The Moulin Rouge closed in October 1955, perhaps due to poor management, although suspicions lingered that the Strip properties arranged their shows in a way that would draw business away from the African American establishment. The Moulin Rouge later reopened under new management, which subsequently excluded African Americans. On March 25, 1960, an important meeting attended by leaders from the NAACP, *Las Vegas Sun* publisher Hank Greenspun, hotel owners, and state and city officials occurred at the Moulin Rouge. To avert strikes and protests, those present took the first steps toward an agreement that would finally integrate the Las Vegas Strip and downtown casinos.[2]

In 2003, an arsonist set fire to the historic Moulin Rouge, burning most of it to the ground. Surviving elements included the front facade and the highly visible tower and sign. All of the distinctive interior elements— the murals, bar, theater, furnishings, and dining area—were gone. In spite of this, the keeper of the National Register of Historic Places insisted that the property continue to be listed, recognizing the value of the few surviving elements and the profoundly important history associated with the building. In May 2009, a fire further damaged it.

MORELLI HOUSE

In 1959, Antonio Morelli, the music director of the Las Vegas Sands Hotel during the 1950s and 1960s, built his dream house bordering on the Desert Inn golf course. It would be another example of southern Nevada inventing the future with its architecture.[3] Morelli was the orchestra leader at a time when the famed Rat Pack—Dean Martin, Frank Sinatra, Sammy Davis Jr., Joey Bishop, and Peter Lawford—were making the stage at the Sands famous. Morelli designed his house with the help of Richard Small, the Desert Inn principal carpenter, and local architect Hugh E. Taylor.

The long building includes roughly thirty-three hundred square feet, with screens composed of open decorative cement block. The roof is covered in white rock to reflect sunlight and help cool the house. With its overall low massing, the Morelli House represented a departure from the more conventional ranch-style homes of the period. As architectural historian Alan Hess indicates, the two-bedroom Morelli House features "clean lines, flat roofs, glass walls and spacious, open interiors . . . emblematic of 1950s modern design found in all Sunbelt cities."[4] This was a house for the future.

In 1978, Kay Glenn, Howard Hughes's personal secretary for a quarter of a century, purchased the house from Morelli's widow, Antonio having died in 1974. In 2001, Glenn sold it to casino entrepreneur Steve Wynn, who was planning to transform the area into a new hotel-casino development. Fortunately, Glenn and Wynn recognized the Morelli House had value, and so they worked with the Junior League of Las Vegas to have the structure moved and preserved. In 2001, the Junior League relocated the building to Ninth Street and Bridger Avenue, where it now serves as a cultural center.[5]

The Morelli House exhibits a remarkable degree of preservation that

Antonio Morelli, the music director of the Sands Hotel, built his state-of-the-art house in 1959. The Junior League of Las Vegas moved the building to its present location in 2001.

extends to interior features, including futuristic light fixtures. A stone wall serves as the backdrop for a dramatic fireplace hood extending to the ceiling and made of pleated copper. Original appliances, selected by Morelli because they were state of the art and ultramodern for the time, still include instruction booklets. Replacement furnishings have been provided by Vladimir Kagan, known internationally for his modern furniture designs during the mid-twentieth century. Kagan served the restoration as the house's lead interior designer and has arranged pieces consistent with the period and with the Morellis' sense of futuristic styles. Opened in 2007, the Morelli House typifies a forward-looking Las Vegas in the mid-twentieth century. Constructed when the city was growing into its role as an international icon, the house, like Las Vegas itself, anticipated the future, unbounded by previous or contemporary conventions.

LA CONCHA MOTEL

Like the Morelli House, the La Concha Motel in Las Vegas is ultramodern, but it also turned away from the convention of building with straight edges and right angles. The clamshell lobby, the surviving part of the historic structure, has an undulating roofline with low points almost touching the ground and then rising to a trio of peaks soaring twenty-eight feet high. Paul Revere Williams, the African American architect mentioned before as the designer of the First Church of Christ, Scientist, in Reno, provided plans for this innovative building, which dates to 1961.

The La Concha Motel was augmented by a hotel in 1974, but the lobby continued to serve until 2004, when it closed. Eventually, casino mogul Steve Wynn transformed the site into "Wynn," yet another of his high-rise properties. Fortunately, the Neon Museum of Las Vegas was able to obtain the lobby. The museum had been in search of a facility to act as a visitors center for its popular neon-sign "boneyard," and the La Concha was a perfect fit. The organization subsequently moved the distinctive hotel lobby, giving it a second life for the community. The historic structure speaks, like the signs themselves, to the avant-garde nature of Las Vegas design.

Paul Revere Williams designed the La Concha Motel lobby in 1961. The futuristic expression of architecture is now sited at the Neon Museum "boneyard" to serve as an interpretive center.

FLEISCHMANN ATMOSPHERIUM PLANETARIUM

Reno's Fleischmann Atmospherium Planetarium was completed only two years after the La Concha, and like its southern Nevada counterpart, it represents a radical departure from conventional design. Funding for the project came from the Fleischmann Foundation, established by the estate of Max C. Fleischmann (1877–1951). Situated in a part of the state not noted for being ultramodern, the Atmospherium Planetarium nevertheless epitomizes all that is futuristic, and visitors have revered the place since it opened in 1963. At that time, local residents celebrated the fact that Reno, in spite of its limited population, possessed a venue of this sort, and most regarded its architecture as a beautiful expression of a time when the nation was hurtling itself into space and a race to the moon. The

Reno's Fleischmann Atmospherium Planetarium, opened in 1963, was the first of its kind in the world.

fact that this was the world's first facility to combine the function of an atmospherium (projecting daytime skies) with that of a planetarium (featuring nighttime star fields) was probably lost on most. What mattered was that this was a cutting-edge expression of a society looking to a future in the space age, and it was bringing an era of invention and exploration to Nevada.

O. Richard Norton, the first director of the Atmospherium Planetarium, invented the concept of a sky dome combining the ability of projecting day and night skies. This was in part to answer the needs of the Desert Research Institute, which developed the property. Founded in 1959, the institute is dedicated to the study of the desert environment, including its weather. Projecting daytime skies and in particular weather patterns was a way of letting the public know of the institute's groundbreaking work. Norton, however, understood that a dome with a projection system for daytime images could also serve as a backdrop for stars, and so he combined the functions.[6] Planetariums had become increasingly popular since the first one in the nation opened in Chicago in 1930. Only thirty years later, planners worked in Reno to implement an innovation that proponents hoped would widen the appeal of this type of theater.

Raymond Hellmann, a northern Nevada architect, intended the Atmospherium Planetarium to be a radical departure from conventional design. The single-pour 180-ton concrete roof is in the shape of a modified hyperbolic paraboloid, or as the *Nevada State Journal* reported in 1963, "that is to say, a cross section of the roof in one direction is an hyperbola and at right angles a parabola."[7] Put another way, the roof swoops up at its peaks, front and back, and with a graceful turn down touches the ground for support at the two sides, providing the structure with its distinctive "butterfly" appearance. Exterior walls are coated with a sea-green mortar embedded with small white rocks.

Inside, an experimental air-based solar heating and cooling system failed, but the inventive design foreshadowed later water-based efforts in the technology. Because the floor-to-ceiling rotating panels—black on one side and white on the other—remain inside the forty-foot-tall windows of the south elevation, they add to the remarkable look of the building both from the interior and from the outside. The thirty-foot dome dominates the large open space inside, which wraps itself around this central function. Steel cables strung in straight lines in the futuristic balustrades form hyperbolic paraboloids, curves echoing the roof and crafted with "string art," a style popular at the time.

Ultimately, the Fleischmann Atmospherium Planetarium has struggled to survive since it opened, and the innovation it represented proved less than successful. The Desert Research Institute quickly balked at the expense of operating the outlet for its research. The planetarium function proved far more popular than the ability of the theater to project clouds, and photographing daytime skies was expensive with a special fish-eye-lens motion-picture camera. Under the threat of closing the facility, the institute moved management of the Atmospherium Planetarium to the University of Nevada–Reno. Although the community raised funds for an endowment, it proved too little, and the university was forced to subsidize its operation. The university found little inspiration to assist a program that served the public more than its students, and so the facility continued to exist as something as an orphan, eventually abandoning its atmospherium function and that part of its name, even though the legacy of innovation is what grants the facility national significance.[8]

In 2002, university president John Lilley indicated he would tear down the planetarium, but the outcry was so great he was forced to relent, and there are those who suggest he never recovered politically from his assault on the popular facility. The theater has remained the ever-popular institution it was when first opened in 1963. Operations may continue to be a struggle, but the planetarium is a community favorite, and it is easy to imagine that its signature style of architecture is one of the reasons.[9]

PIONEER THEATER–AUDITORIUM

Unlike the Fleischmann Atmospherium Planetarium, the futuristic architecture of Reno's Pioneer Center for the Performing Arts has often been an object of criticism. Since its opening, the metal geodesic dome has been known as the golden turtle. The futuristic structure was a provocative experiment, but it replaced the old State Building, a distinguished expression of turn-of-the-century architecture, and not everyone regarded the transition as an improvement. Regardless of occasional disapproval, the design of the Pioneer Center is remarkable, winning it recognition from the National Register of Historic Places when it was less than forty years old.

The Oklahoma architectural firm of Bozalis, Dickinson, and Roloff designed the Pioneer Theater-Auditorium, which was completed in 1967. A concrete plaza featuring a statue of a pioneer family replaced grounds of trees and shaded lawn. The statue stood before the previous State Building, but it was reused, and it became the inspiration for the name of the

The Pioneer Theater-Auditorium, completed in Reno in 1967, features a striking metal geodesic dome.

new facility. On the east end of the plaza, the theater rises with concrete walls supporting the five hundred faceted, gold-anodized aluminum panels. The signature rounded dome spans 140 feet. Inside, the main floor of the theater has 987 seats, and the balcony holds another 513, making this the largest theater in northern Nevada. Problems with acoustics and sight lines, however, limited the value of all the seats.

The Pioneer Theater-Auditorium was not the first expression of modernism in the region, but it was one of the largest and most striking monumental structures in this style. Temcor installed the dome. Don Rickter, the cofounder of the company, was a student of Buckminster Fuller, who promoted the idea of using geodesic domes. Temcor had installed domes throughout the nation, making them the obvious contractor for the theater. The geodesic dome takes advantage of the ability of the various panels to lock into position quickly, efficiently distributing the weight of the structure across the foundation. Beginning in the 1950s, this innovation in building design has inspired many to use it as an alternative to conventional squared structures, and geodesic domes stepped easily into the menu of possibilities for modernism.

For the first decades, the Pioneer proved less than a financial success. In 1988, the Reno-Sparks Convention and Visitors Authority, which managed the facility, reached an agreement with the Reno Performing Arts Center Association, a collation of arts and other groups, to assume control. The theater was subsequently known as the Pioneer Center for the Performing Arts. It has seen many distinguished entertainers over the years and remains the principal large theater in northern Nevada. Although the architecture is odd, it has lent the institution an easily recognized facade.

THESE SIX STRUCTURES collectively define postwar Nevada as it adjusted to a new international role, anticipating the future. Recognition of this period as historic has developed slowly with the passing of decades, but it is increasingly clear to most that these sorts of resources speak to one of the most important eras in the history of the state. During this period, Nevada transformed into a tourism oddity, formulating a new persona and offering diversions some sought but few places tolerated. By the end of the 1960s, the state had become a world leader in gaming and large-scale entertainment tourism. Its architecture looked toward a future its developers were inventing.

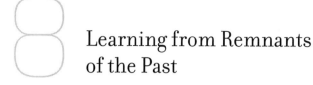

Learning from Remnants of the Past

Throughout the course of Nevada history, an unremarkable structure has endured. The simple adobe at the Kiel Ranch may or may not be the oldest building in the state. Between fact and folklore, the past remains vaguely defined. In spite of its age and the formidable obstacles confronting preservationists, the modest structure still stands. The story of its survival illuminates the challenges confronted by those seeking to preserve the material remnants of the past.

The challenge presented by the Kiel Ranch adobe echoes the dubious prospects confronting many of Nevada's historic structures. For the most part, the buildings discussed in this book are flourishing today as cultural centers or are about to assume this role. Their good fortune was predicated upon the persistence of local preservationists who refused to let them go as well as upon financial assistance from the Commission for Cultural Affairs. If not for this intervention, most would have been lost. As the fate of the Kiel Ranch White House and many of its outbuildings shows, every historic building is only one disaster away from oblivion. And of course, extinction still threatens the old adobe. The state's historic buildings are nonrenewable resources. Their futures cannot be taken for granted.

The adobe walls of the Kiel Ranch are showing stress and will not last much longer without a great deal of assistance.

Many of these venerable structures survived because people drew on a cultural frame of reference that encouraged the use of scarce resources. Confronted with an austere environment and limited assets, the men and women who built Nevada were loath to abandon a building. They found novel ways, therefore, to conserve their structures. Survival in Nevada has always been linked to inventiveness. Yet even an ingenious imagination cannot prevent a fire or an earthquake from destroying a building. In an instant, a photograph can become the only surviving evidence of how a work of architecture once expressed a social and cultural mind-set.

The Nevada legislature's creation of the Commission for Cultural

Affairs can in itself be seen as an example of an audacious spirit that cobbles together solutions from unlikely parts. The commission emerged with no paid staff, relying instead on assistance from existing employees. Trimming overhead to nothing allowed the state to experiment with a bond-funded program geared toward preserving historic structures and transforming them into cultural centers. As the years passed, it became evident that the program had a dramatic, positive effect on the state's cultural setting, especially as it related to education and tourism. It is also true, however, that the commission experienced several setbacks, but adversity is not unfamiliar to Nevadans. They learned long ago that the price of inventiveness is occasional failure, and the birth of the commission was a journey into the possibilities of trial-and-error methodology. Like the state that generated it, however, the agency persevered.

When the state legislature first entertained the idea of launching the Commission for Cultural Affairs, it had reason to be optimistic about the efficacy of a comprehensive approach to the development of the state's cultural resources. The successful restoration of Virginia City's historic Fourth Ward School and its transformation into a regional cultural center pointed the way. Cooperation among a number of state agencies and local volunteers was central to the institution's success. Assisted by the Nevada State Museum, the Nevada Humanities Committee, and the State Historic Preservation Office, Storey County opened a museum on the school's first floor in 1986.[1] Thanks to this achievement, the building still stands, representing a benchmark not only for education in nineteenth-century Nevada but also for the state's twentieth-century cultural development. Imagination and teamwork preserved the distinguished historic building and pressed it into service, opening its doors to residents and tourists alike. In the 1980s, the proud old school became an example of how a cooperative, unified approach could amplify the effect of experts, local volunteers, and limited funds.

The Fourth Ward School served as an early flagship for the Commission for Cultural Affairs. Those who argued that Nevada needed a statewide bond program pointed to the Virginia City museum as an example of what could

The bullet-shaped dome of the Nye County Courthouse rises amid the town of Tonopah. Dozens of restored buildings enjoy new roles, contributing to their communities.

be achieved with minimal funding and maximum cooperation. The school in turn benefited from commission funding, and the successive opening of each of its floors to public access has underscored the broad commitment of the State of Nevada and Virginia City not just to preserving the school but also to using it as a cultural center.

Whereas the successful rehabilitation of the Fourth Ward School constituted a positive inducement for the creation of the Commission for Cultural Affairs, the tragic demolition of one of the state's finest historic resources also encouraged the founding of the agency. The Virginia and Truckee Shops in Carson City stood unused for decades, even though the structure's mighty stone walls contained enormous potential for economic development and tourism. Days before the opening of the 1991 legislative session, the property owner demolished the building, presumably thinking that an open lot would attract development dollars. The land remains unused. The loss of one of the nation's finest railroad resources inflamed state legislators, and accusations flew concerning who was at fault. A turning point occurred when Yerington's Joe Dini, Speaker of the assembly, asked during a meeting of the Ways and Means Committee, "So, what could you achieve if we actually gave you some money?" The answer was the Commission for Cultural Affairs, an innovative solution continuing a fine Nevada tradition of working with whatever was available.[2]

Over a decade and a half, commission funding has had far-reaching effects throughout the state. Local groups wove together public funds, volunteers, and other resources to save and use historic structures. Many of these solutions involved moving buildings, an alternative generally scorned by preservationists throughout the nation. Moving deprives a historic resource of its context, challenging visitors as they attempt to understand the relationship of a building to its past. Nevertheless, placing a structure in a new location sometimes represents the only option, and some remnants of the past are too valuable to lose.

The wandering buildings of Reno's Ferretto Ranch underscore the benefit of conserving historic resources in pragmatic ways. The well-traveled Ferretto structures thrive in their new setting as symbols of change but also of continuity with Nevada's agricultural past. Had they not been moved first once and then finally to the Bartley Ranch Park, they would have been irretrievably lost.

Similarly, purists advocated keeping resources like the Las Vegas railroad cottages on their original sites, but realistically, property owners could not be expected to maintain modest homes on land with as much potential for dramatic financial gain as exists in southern Nevada. One by one, these cottages were demolished until the only viable option for the few survivors was to remove them. Otherwise, they too would have been destroyed.[3] After the turn of the twenty-first century, the Clark County Museum moved a railroad

Dan Braddock is one of hundreds of volunteers who have contributed tens of thousands of hours, restoring dozens of buildings. He tends the soda fountain at his beloved McGill Drugstore, which he helped turn into an interpretive center.

cottage to its facility in Henderson, providing an opportunity to preserve and interpret this early period of Nevada history for future generations. The cinder-block construction made moving the house particularly problematic. Nevertheless, the museum accomplished its goal, and it is possible to see a type of architecture that played an important role in the history of the state. Indeed, the Clark County facility has provided a home to many orphaned historic buildings, and several of these resources benefited from Commission for Cultural Affairs funding.

The historic Whitehead House of Las Vegas provides another example of a building moving to be saved. In 1996, it became the property of the Oxford Group, which needed the real estate for a parking garage. The company planned to demolish the house and erect a new structure in its place. The Junior League of Las Vegas wanted to save the building for use as the organization's headquarters, but it could not pay a sufficient price to fore-stall the home's destruction. In March 1997, a contractor arrived to knock down the Whitehead House. Confronted by a bulldozer with engine running, Louise Helton, the league's representative, Las Vegas city councilman Mat-thew Callister, and Plaza Hotel owner Jackie Gaughan appeared at the site and negotiated a temporary reprieve for the old house. Shortly after that, council-men Arnie Adamsen and Gary Reese became involved in the effort to save the building, and the various interested parties struck a deal to save the resource. The league moved the building to a temporary site, thus freeing the lot for development by the corporation. At the same time, the league began raising funds to purchase a new lot for the structure using grants from the Commis-sion for Cultural Affairs.

In July 2000, just as the Junior League had reached its financial goal and was prepared to move the Whitehead House to its permanent location, the structure fell victim to a fire apparently caused by vagrants. The home had figured prominently in Nevada history, and its loss was tragic, but once it had ceased to fulfill its original function, the house's survival was threatened. The league offered the Whitehead House its best chance for survival, but even that noble effort was not enough.[4] The sad story concluded, nevertheless, with an upbeat epilogue. The league took on the preservation of the Morelli House, now sited on the property originally acquired for the Whitehead House.

The lobby for the La Concha Hotel of Las Vegas was also successfully moved. Its 2006 relocation to the Neon Museum was no mean feat, since the lobby's thin concrete shell had been poured over a web of reinforced steel, creating a structure that was not meant to travel. Because of its height—nearly a dozen feet taller than the freeway underpass in its path—the build-ing needed to be cut up for transportation, adding to the complexity of the undertaking. In a community noted for the demolition of its historic archi-tecture, saving the La Concha lobby was an important success, and it under-scores the increasing awareness of the importance of history and culture in the world's premier postmodern city.

Numerous other examples of moving historic resources to save them include the Marvel Ranch cookhouse in Battle Mountain, the Richardson House in Winnemucca, the Southern Pacific Railroad Depot in Lovelock, Reno's twice-moved Lake Mansion, the twice-moved Glendale School in Sparks, and Sherman Station in the City of Elko. Although moving a structure is never preferred, it can be pragmatic. Indeed, the idea of relocating buildings is a historic Nevada tradition. The Gold Hill Depot incorporated a construction shed moved to its current location in 1869. The Foreman-Roberts House in Carson City began its life in the heart of Washoe Valley before heading south in the 1870s. In addition, earlier generations of Fernley residents moved their East End School to its current location when they chose to "recycle" that structure. Nevadans learned long ago that the key to success in the state's real estate market was flexibility, not location. The value of a building no longer useful at one place often demanded its move to another. The state's unforgiving environment bred a pragmatism that would not allow for the waste of built resources. This tradition reverberates in the origin of many of the state's cultural centers.

Finding the right land for a building, however, is only one of the issues that has challenged those wishing to preserve and use historic structures. Supporters of St. Augustine's Catholic Church in Austin found an obstacle to their preservation efforts in the state constitution, which prohibits awarding public funds to religious institutions. The question was resolved when the Catholic diocese transferred ownership of the property to a private nonprofit organization, making the building eligible for grants and available to the community for a variety of uses. Because the structure endured years of deterioration, the new owner quickly secured the structure from the elements to make certain its service to the community would continue.

Another example of piecing together resources to create imaginative solutions occurred in Reno when it declared the existence of an arts corridor along the Truckee River. By fusing various arts organizations and events together with buildings, a new focus was possible that brought historic sites

FACING PAGE:
The interior of the Bethel African Methodist Episcopal Church is newly refinished and ready to serve Reno with performances and exhibits.

to the forefront. During the last quarter of the twentieth century, Reno's downtown area, like so many others across the country, had declined. In an attempt to reverse this process, the city reinvented itself by supporting the arts. Working closely with local groups, the city enhanced its downtown and bolstered its tourism industry by developing an arts, theater, and entertainment district along the Truckee River. Reno planners concluded that tourists who came to Reno to gamble might extend their stays if they were offered a wide variety of artistic and cultural experiences. At the same time, the city hoped to enrich the lives of local residents, and so it began developing a cultural corridor extending from the California Building in Idlewild Park on Reno's west end to its Automobile Museum on the city's east side. Tapping into its cultural heritage, the corridor was to include several of Reno's most interesting historic structures. Four of these became projects of the Commission for Cultural Affairs: the California Building; Riverside Hotel; First Church of Christ, Scientist; and McKinley Park School.[5]

A similar undertaking occurred to the south. In 2002, after lengthy

negotiations and with the help of Senator Harry Reid, the federal General Services Administration transferred the title of the post office to the City of Las Vegas. A lease allowed the Postal Service to continue operating there until 2004, when it moved its services to other locations. At that point, the task of restoration began in earnest. The project promised to cost tens of millions of dollars, and the city, at every point of the decision-making process, demonstrated a commitment to executing the restoration of the important structure to the highest possible standard. Extensive analysis in the courtroom, for example, revealed that bland cream-colored paint had covered what were once lively color schemes to enhance details. This gave experts the opportunity to return the room to its original appearance.

The project will take several years to complete, but ultimately it promises to be the southern Nevada flagship of preservation, serving as the focus of a cultural district in the heart of a city known more for its gambling, its Mafia past, and its sins. In part because of commission encouragement, one of the state's more significant structures will return to service as a museum. The location of hearings intent on breaking the power of the Mafia will in turn present the history of the Mob and its relationship to Las Vegas. Perhaps its most important function will be to interpret the enigmatic past of a community that holds the world's fascination.

Some of the greatest challenges faced project proponents of younger resources. There are problems and promises associated with historic preservation in a rapidly developing state like Nevada. Of the six structures representing the modern period, one burned and another failed as a cultural center. Fortunately, four have more promising futures, but two had to be moved from their original sites in order to be saved. These more recent additions serve as examples of how attempts at preservation can, on occasion, fail to resist the forces that sometimes obliterate the vestiges of the recent past.

Plans exist to reconstruct the Moulin Rouge, a hotel-casino noted for its place in southern Nevada's African American culture, using its charred surviving elements, but progress remains elusive. Similarly, the fate of the Huntridge Theater is yet to be determined. Some maintained that the opening of the Las Vegas Hard Rock Hotel-Casino and other similar venues with stages for rock concerts forced the Huntridge to compete in a new environment. For whatever reason, the Huntridge became a lost cause, as the historic theater failed to survive when faced with glitzy new stages and the clout of well-funded corporations.[6]

During the time the Huntridge Theater was open, it served hundreds of thousands. In addition, grants from the Commission for Cultural Affairs placed covenants on the structure that can leverage the preservation of the building for a while. It is possible to imagine a time when the theater will reopen to the public. At the same time, it may be demolished eventually. When events conspire to cause the destruction of a historic building, too often the loss cannot be prevented.

Dozens of commission projects illustrate how Nevadans, both past and present, have used their creativity and imagination as they drew upon scarce

Dancers bring life to the stage of Piper's Opera House, newly restored and promising to serve the twenty-first century just as it did the previous two.

resources to forge the state's material culture. Miners, ranchers, innkeepers, craftsmen, civil servants, and many others created and then re-created a distinctly Nevada culture in the lands lying east of the Sierra Nevada and west of the Goshute, Snake, and Virgin mountains. As demonstrated by the state's architecture, this culture celebrates experimentation, a certain playfulness, and innovation. Civilization is always new in Nevada. As a result, the state constantly exhibits a youthful air. Its freewheeling moral ambivalence and openness to innovation—characteristics typifying contemporary Las Vegas—are the logical outcome of continuous and necessary invention in an unrelenting environment. Nevadans have always struggled to construct havens of sociability and culture in places ranging from remote desert locations to sophisticated urban centers.

The restoration efforts recounted in these pages simply represent the most recent chapters in stories involving a wide spectrum of historic resources. Their tales began decades ago—or in some cases, even more than a century earlier—and in each instance, the architectural styles and artistic aspirations encapsulated within these buildings set the stage for a narrative involving inventiveness and success with limited resources. Buildings that typified the Nevada adaptation to an unforgiving landscape survive to remind subsequent generations that the true test of living in the state is not in how it can be made to look like someplace else. Instead, the challenge has been to transform an often harsh setting into a celebration of humanity and a glorification of the state's mountains, its river valleys, and its deserts, lands that were once derisively described as the nation's "wastes."

Notes

Research on the buildings discussed in this book relied heavily on hundreds of grant applications submitted by project proponents. In addition, most of these buildings are listed in the State or National Register of Historic Places, and these nominations also served as valuable sources of information. Portions of this book are based on a manuscript developed by Elizabeth Safford Harvey titled "Art, Enlightenment, Culture: A Retrospective History of the Commission for Cultural Affairs" (2001). Although not cited individually here, the authors acknowledge these important documents, which are on file in Carson City, Nevada, at the State Historic Preservation Office.

INTRODUCTION

1. See Russell R. Elliott, *The Turn of the Century Mining Boom.*

1 ■ A TERRITORY OF HUMBLE BEGINNINGS

1. For a discussion of the frontier and especially of Turner's controversial view of the West, see Frederick Jackson Turner, "The Significance of the Frontier in American History" and "The Problem of the West." See also Ray Allen Billington, *Frederick Jackson Turner: Historian, Scholar, Teacher;* Allan G. Bogue, *Frederick Jackson Turner: Strange Roads Going Down;* and John Mack Faragher, "'A Nation Thrown Back Upon Itself': Frederick Jackson Turner and the Frontier," 1–10.

2. Sally Zanjani, *Devils Will Reign: How Nevada Began.*

3. Faragher, "'A Nation Thrown Back Upon Itself,'" 9; Frederick Jackson Turner, "The Significance of the Section in American History," 214.

4. Richard F. Burton, *The City of the Saints, and Across the Rocky Mountains to California,* 509.

5. Richard Gordon Lillard, *Desert Challenge: An Interpretation of Nevada,* 75.

6. James W. Hulse, *The Silver State: Nevada's Heritage Reinterpreted,* 39–41, 187–89.

7. Ibid., 187; Stanley W. Paher, *Las Vegas: As It Began—as It Grew.*

8. A. D. Hopkins, "John C. Frémont," in *The First 100: Portraits of the Men and Women Who Shaped Las Vegas,* edited by A. D. Hopkins and K. J. Evans, 2–3; Harold A. Steiner, "The Old Spanish Trail, 1829–1850"; Terri McBride, *Exploration and Early Settlement in Nevada.*

9. Zanjani, *Devils Will Reign*; A. D. Hopkins, "William Bringhurst," in *First 100*, edited by Hopkins and Evans, 6–7.

10. K. J. Evans, "O. D. Gass," in *First 100*, edited by Hopkins and Evans, 8.

11. The name also appears as Kyle. Contrary to standard German pronunciation, *Kiel* is pronounced with a long *i*. Historic American Buildings Survey, "Kiel Ranch, North Las Vegas, Nevada," on file at the State Historic Preservation Office, Carson City.

12. Jim W. Steely, senior historical consultant with SWCA Environmental Consultants, interview, October 14, 2008. Steely was preparing a plan for the Kiel Ranch on behalf of the City of North Las Vegas. Thanks to Steely for his assistance.

13. Paher, *Las Vegas*, 57; K. J. Evans, "Helen Stewart," in *First 100*, edited by Hopkins and Evans, 12.

14. Mella Rothwell Harmon and Guy L. Rocha, "Foreman-Roberts House." The Nevada State Historic Preservation Office National Register of Historic Places files assert the 1859 date and then provide the 1863 correction.

15. Zanjani, *Devils Will Reign*.

16. The Winters Ranch also incorporated Egyptian Revival elements (Julie Nicoletta, *Buildings of Nevada*, 87). Members of the Roberts family lived in their Carson City home until 1969, when the youngest of the Roberts children, Thurman Roberts, died and bequeathed the property to the State of Nevada. The state turned the house over to Carson City, and since the structure needed extensive repairs, the city concluded that demolition was the only reasonable option. Nevertheless, the community rose up in defense of the aged house, and the Nevada Landmarks Society formed for the specific purpose of saving the house and converting it into a Victorian-period museum and park.

17. Zanjani, *Devils Will Reign*.

18. Ronald M. James, *Temples of Justice: County Courthouses of Nevada*, 57.

19. Ibid., 59–60; Marlena Hellwinkel, "Memo to Elizabeth Safford Harvey," 2002, on file at the State Historic Preservation Office, Carson City.

2 ■ A STATE OF INTERNATIONAL FAME

1. The concept of an emergent culture is discussed in Raymond Williams, *Marxism and Literature*, 122–27. For the early development of what would become Nevada, see Zanjani, *Devils Will Reign*; and Ronald M. James, *The Roar and the Silence: A History of Virginia City and the Comstock Lode*.

2. On the discovery of gold, see Hubert Howe Bancroft, *The Works of Hubert Howe Bancroft*, 25:93; and Dayton Historic Society, "Gold!! The Key to Dayton's Discovery," http://www.dayton-valley.org/gold.htm. On Dayton as the first settlement, see Martin Griffith, "What's Nevada's Oldest Town?"; and Guy Rocha, "Nevada's First Permanent Settlement," http://www.cmla.clan.lib.nv.us/docs/nsla/archives/myth/myth22.htm.

3. Dayton Historic Society, "The Legend and Lore of Dayton's History," http://www.dayton-valley.org/gold.htm.

4. Laura Tenant, interview by Elizabeth Safford Harvey, 2002, audiotape on file at the State Historic Preservation Office, Carson City.

5. Joe Curtis, telephone communication, September 11, 2002, notes on file at the State Historic Preservation Office, Carson City.

6. Steven R. Frady, *Jump Her Lively, Boys: An Introduction to the Fire Departments of the Comstock Lode*, 18.

7. R. James, *Roar and Silence*, 78–85; David F. Myrick, *Railroads of Nevada and Eastern California*, 1:136–62; Ted Wurm and Harre Demoro, *The Silver Short Line: A History of the Virginia and Truckee Railroad*.

8. *Territorial Enterprise*, March 16, 1876; Lee Lukes Pickering, *The Story of St. Mary's Art Center Now and St. Mary Louise Hospital Then*, 9–11.

9. Pickering, *Story of St. Mary's Art Center*, 13; *Nevada Appeal*, September 12, 1984.

10. *Territorial Enterprise*, October 15, 1876.

11. R. James, *Roar and Silence*, 195; Susan A. James, *Virginia City's Historic Fourth Ward School: From Pride to Glory*.

12. Donald R. Abbe, *Austin and the Reese River Mining District*; Oscar Lewis, *The Town That Died Laughing: The Story of Austin, Nevada, Rambunctious Early-Day Mining Camp and of Its Renowned Newspaper, the "Reese River Reveille."*

13. R. James, *Temples of Justice*; James W. Hulse, *Lincoln County, Nevada, 1864–1909: History of a Mining Region*.

14. Hulse, *Silver State*, 128–29.

15. R. James, *Temples of Justice*, 115.

16. Hulse, *Silver State*, 128–29; R. James, *Temples of Justice*, 113–18.

17. Sally Zanjani and Guy Louis Rocha, *The Ignoble Conspiracy: Radicalism on Trial in Nevada*, 29.

18. Hulse, *Silver State*, 333–35.

19. Susan A. James, "Shakespeare and Bear Fights."

20. Some local insistence that Houdini appeared on the stage is yet to be set aside completely, but lacking evidence, it is only possible to conclude that he was not there.

21. Ibid., 21.

22. For a history on the institution and John Piper, see ibid. See also Piper's Opera House, *Bringing Piper's Into the 21st Century*, 2–3.

3 ■ THE OTHER EARLY NEVADA

1. Don D. Fowler and David B. Madsen, "Prehistory of the Southeastern Area," 175–79; William D. Rowley, "Ranching and Farming in Nevada," 3, on file at the State Historic Preservation Office, Carson City.

2. Rowley, "Ranching and Farming," 3–4.

3. Helen S. Carlson, *Place Names of Nevada: A Geographic Dictionary*; John M. Gomes, "Golconda's Glory Days, 1898–1910."

4. For the early Truckee Meadows, see Edwin Bryant, *What I Saw in California*. For the Carson Valley, see Elisha D. Perkins, "Truckee Meadows Trail" (1849), as quoted in http://www.donnerpartydiary.com/truckmdw.htm. For a general history, see N. A. Hummel, *General History and Resources of Washoe County, Nevada*, 4–7.

5. Thomas Wren, *A History of the State of Nevada: Its Resources and People*, 637–38; Anna B. Koval and Katherine Boyne, *Peter Dalton Ranch (Joseph Ferretto Ranch)*, 13–14, on file at the State Historic Preservation Office, Carson City.

6. Koval and Boyne, *Peter Dalton Ranch*, 15–16.

7. Sparks Sertoma and La Sertoma, *Historic Glendale School House*, n.d., brochure, photocopy on file at the State Historic Preservation Office, Carson City.

8. The history of the school and its addition can be deduced from historic photographs available in the Glendale School National Register of Historic Places nomination file at the State Historic Preservation Office, Carson City. See also Natalie D. Peters, "The American One-Room Schoolhouse: A Study of a Community Vernacular Building Artifact."

9. Sparks Sertoma and La Sertoma, *Historic Glendale School House*, n.p. For Senator McCarran, see Jerome E. Edwards, *Patrick McCarran: Political Boss of Nevada*.

10. Tom Burrous, interview by Elizabeth Safford Harvey, 2001; Tom Burrous and James H. Ringer, interview by Elizabeth Safford Harvey, 2001, audiotapes on file at the State Historic Preservation Office, Carson City.

11. *Reno Gazette-Journal*, July 17, 2004.

12. Louise Walther Botsford, "Valentine Walther"; Edna Patterson, Louise A. Ulph, and Victor Goodwin, *Nevada's Northeast Frontier*, 449–51.

13. Elko Chamber of Commerce brochure, n.d., on file at the State Historic Preservation Office, Carson City; *Reno Gazette-Journal*, August 24, 1997.

14. Elaine Barkdull, interview by Elizabeth Safford Harvey, 2001, audiotape on file at the State Historic Preservation Office, Carson City.

15. Francis H. Leavitt, "The Influence of the Mormon People in the Settlement of Clark County," 67–68; Juanita Brooks, *Dudley Leavitt: Pioneer to Southern Utah*, 49–52, 79; W. Paul Reeve, "The Virgin River Doused Cotton Mission Settlers' Hopes"; Carolyn Gratton-Aiello, "New St. Joseph, Nevada: The Muddy Mission Experience Revisited," 31; Pearson Starr Corbett, "Settling the Muddy River Valley."

16. Brooks, *Dudley Leavitt*, 75–76, 79–82; F. Leavitt, "Influence of the Mormon People," 123–48; Leonard J. Arrington, Feramorz Y. Fox, and Dean L. May, *Building the City of God: Community and Cooperation Among the Mormons*, 306–8; Violet Leavitt, "The History of the Virgin Valley," 248.

17. Correspondence from the Virgin Valley Heritage Museum to Elizabeth Safford Harvey, 2004, on file at the State Historic Preservation Office, Carson City.

18. *Historical Walking Tour* (Mesquite, Nev.: City of Mesquite, n.d.). See also *Structural Evaluation Report for "the Old Rock House"* (City of Mesquite: Western Design Group, 2005), both on file at the State Historic Preservation Office, Carson City.

19. *Las Vegas Sun*, December 12, 2000.

20. Dean Heller, *Political History of Nevada*; Hulse, *Lincoln County*.

21. Myron Angel, *History of Nevada, 1881*, 487; Leonard Arrington and Richard Jensen, "Panaca: Mormon Outpost Among the Mining Camps"; Hulse, *Silver State*, 94.

22. Phyllis Robistow, interviews by Elizabeth Safford Harvey, 2001 and 2002, audiotapes on file at the State Historic Preservation Office, Carson City.

23. Hulse, *Silver State*, 122; Russell McDonald, "The Development of Lovelock."

24. Hulse, *Silver State*, 330.

25. Doris Cerveri, *With Curry's Compliments: The Story of Abraham Curry, Founder of Nevada's Capital City and Father of the Carson City Mint*.

26. Arnold A. Millard, *History of the Carson Brewing Company: "Nevada's Oldest Business"*; Angel, *History of Nevada, 1881*, 550–57; *Reno Gazette-Journal*, July 5, 1997; C. W. Torrence, *History of Masonry in Nevada*.

27. *Reno Gazette-Journal*, July 5, 1997.

28. Angel, *History of Nevada, 1881*, 192.

29. Ibid., 205.

30. Wilda Oldham, *Carson City: Nevada's Capital City*, 167–68.

1. Elliott, *Turn of the Century Mining Boom*, is the definitive work on this period.

2. Carlson, *Place Names of Nevada*, 247–48.

3. R. James, *Temples of Justice*, 87.

4. Ronald M. James, "Defining the Group: Nineteenth-Century Cornish on the Mining Frontier"; Ronald M. James, "Home Away From Home: Cornish Immigrants in Nineteenth-Century Nevada"; A. L. Rowse, *The Cousin Jacks: The Cornish in America*; Cecil Todd, *The Cornish Miner in America*.

5. Elliott, *Turn of the Century Mining Boom*, 3–8; Russell R. Elliott with the assistance of William D. Rowley, *History of Nevada*, 211–12.

6. R. James, *Temples of Justice*; Shawn Hall, *A Guide to the Ghost Towns and Mining Camps of Nye County, Nevada*; Hulse, *History of Nevada*, 165–66; Elliott with Rowley, *History of Nevada*, 338–40.

7. *Las Vegas Review-Journal*, October 20, 2006.

8. Hulse, *History of Nevada*, 336.

9. R. James, *Temples of Justice*, 121–24.

10. James D. Van Trump, "The Romanesque Revival in Pittsburg," 22. See also Carrol L. V. Meeks, "Romanesque Before Richardson in the United States." H. H. Richardson, in particular, developed the "manliness" inherent to the Romanesque Revival style. See Mark Mumford, "Form Follows Nature: The Origins of American Organic Architecture," 35. For a discussion of Anglo-Saxon mythology associated with the style, see Robin Fleming, "Picturesque History and the Medieval in Nineteenth-Century America."

11. *Tonopah Bonanza*, July 6, 1901; Robert D. McCracken, *A History of Tonopah, Nevada*, 55–57; Mrs. Hugh Brown, *Lady in Boomtown: Miners and Manners on the Nevada Frontier*, 75.

12. Hulse, *Silver State*, 167; Elliott, *Turn of the Century Mining Boom*; Sally Zanjani, *Goldfield: The Last Gold Rush on the Western Frontier*.

13. Elliott with Rowley, *History of Nevada*, 221–23; John B. Reid and Ronald M.

James, *Uncovering Nevada's Past: A Primary Source History of the Silver State*, 90–93; Zanjani and Rocha, *Ignoble Conspiracy*.

14. R. James, *Temples of Justice*, 72.

15. Elizabeth Safford Harvey, "Icon of Community: The Manhattan Schoolhouse."

16. Mella Rothwell Harmon, "Popular Privies Persist," http://dmla.clan.lib. nv.us/docs/dca/thiswas/thiswas17.htm; Mella Rothwell Harmon, "Progressive Privy Program Proved Popular," http://dmla.clan.lib.nv.us/docs/dca/thiswas/thiswas07 .htm. See also Harvey, "Icon of Community." The observation about the Internet and the outhouse is based on testimony given during the 2004 Commission for Cultural Affairs grant hearing.

17. Carlson, *Place Names of Nevada*, 144–45.

18. Shawn Hall, *Old Heart of Nevada: Ghost Towns and Mining Camps of Elko County*; Nicoletta, *Buildings of Nevada*, 163.

19. Helen Wilson, telephone communication, April 25, 2002, notes on file at the State Historic Preservation Office, Carson City.

20. R. James, *Temples of Justice*, 157–58.

21. Hulse, *Silver State*, 174; Elliott, *Turn of the Century Mining Boom*.

22. Hulse, *Silver State*, 174–78; Elliott, *Turn of the Century Mining Boom*.

23. Hulse, *Silver State*, 173, 176–78.

24. Ibid., 132.

25. Elliott with Rowley, *History of Nevada*, 226–30.

26. Elliott, *Turn of the Century Mining Boom*, 229.

27. Dan Robrish, "A Town's Time Capsule."

28. Dan Braddock, telephone communication, September 19, 2001, notes on file at the State Historic Preservation Office, Carson City.

29. Russell R. Elliott, *Growing Up in a Company Town: A Family in the Copper Camp of McGill, Nevada*, 27–30.

30. John M. Townley, *Turn This Water Into Gold: The Story of the Newlands Project*; John M. Townley, *Tough Little Town on the Truckee: Reno, 1868–1900*; Barbara Land and Myrick Land, *A Short History of Reno*; William D. Rowley, *Reno: Hub of the Washoe County*.

31. Hulse, *Silver State*, 197–98.

32. The other survivor is the Mount Rose Elementary School on Arlington Avenue.

33. Ibid., 326–27.

34. Ibid., 125; Hall, *Old Heart of Nevada*.

35. Hulse, *Silver State,* 228–29, 320–21. See also Townley, *Turn This Water Into Gold.*

36. *Fallon Standard,* October 13, 1954.

37. David Igler, *Industrial Cowboys: Miller and Lux and the Transformation of the Far West, 1850–1920,* 4,–5, 150–51.

38. R. James, *Temples of Justice,* 107–12; Hulse, *Silver State,* 178–79, 322.

39. *Yerington Times,* May 18, 1912; Joyce Hollister, "Old School Ties."

40. Hulse, *Silver State,* 127, 135, 319–20; Carson Valley Museum and Cultural Center brochure, n.d., on file at the State Historic Preservation Office, Carson City.

41. "Why Is the 'Wash' Important?" http://www.lvwash.org/important/history /hist_native.html; Hopkins and Evans, *First 100;* Steiner, "Old Spanish Trail."

42. *Las Vegas Sun,* August 10, 2001; Verona Pasquale and Cheryl Rose Crockett, "The End of the Line? The Railroad Cottages of Las Vegas, Then and Now."

5 ■ AFTER THE BOOM

1. Carlson, *Place Names of Nevada,* 47.

2. R. James, *Temples of Justice,* 97.

3. Ibid., 125–32.

4. Myrick, *Railroads of Nevada,* 2:626–62.

5. Hulse, *Silver State,* 180–81.

6. *Sparks Headlight,* January 1991. Numerous articles in the *Sparks Tribune* between 1929 and 1931 chronicle the construction of the building.

7. *Nevada State Journal,* August 22, 1965.

8. "The Riverside," an undocumented report (ca. 2000) on file with the National Register of Historic Places nomination at the State Historic Preservation Office, Carson City.

9. Elliott with Rowley, *History of Nevada,* 108–9; Heller, *Political History of Nevada,* 110–12.

10. Frank Wright, *Wildcat Country: Las Vegas High School and Its Neighborhood, 1930–1945.*

6 ■ A NEW DEAL

1. Jerry Jerrems, "Railroads West: Boulder City Depot Restoration," 1999, report on file at the State Historic Preservation Office, Carson City.

2. *Las Vegas Sun,* June 1, 1980; Dennis McBride, *In the Beginning: A History of Boulder City, Nevada.*

3. *Las Vegas Sun,* June 1, 1980.

4. Elliott with Rowley, *History of Nevada,* 278–85.

5. The date of construction was sometime between 1931 and 1934. Documentation is scarce.

6. Dennis McBride, "Grand Canyon–Boulder Dam Tours, Inc.: Southern Nevada's First Venture Into Commercial Tourism"; *Las Vegas Review-Journal,* March 22, April 4, 1939.

7. Max Bond, "Still Here: Three Architects of Afro-America—Julian Francis Abele, Hilyard Robinson, and Paul R. Williams"; Shashank Bengali, "Williams the Conqueror."

8. Nicholas D. Jackson, "A History of the Stewart Indian School."

9. Although efforts to maintain a museum on the Stewart campus have been fraught with challenges, the overall commitment to have such a center has been the focus of the restoration of two of the structures. With the diverse and complex Stewart building stock, it has been extremely difficult to preserve the campus, but steady progress holds the promise that one of the West's most important historic resources will survive another century.

10. Ronald M. James and Susan A. James, *Castle in the Sky: George Whittell Jr. and the Thunderbird Lodge.*

11. *Nevada Appeal,* December 4, 2000.

12. Ibid.; *Nevada Appeal,* September 22, 2000. The prospect of preserving the deteriorated house seemed limited, but over time, an increasing number of people came to recognize the value of the Stewart Indian School legacy. In the late 1990s, Carson City Parks launched an effort to restore the home, which reopened in 2000 and now serves as a community center.

13. Hulse, *Silver State,* 95–98; Carlson, *Place Names of Nevada,* 156.

14. *Moapa Valley Progress,* September 9, 1998, February 9, 2000; *Las Vegas Review-Journal,* November 11, 1939.

15. Miller also designed a gymnasium in nearby Bunkerville.

16. Ronald M. James and Michelle McFadden, "Remnants of the National Youth Administration in Nevada."

7 ■ INVENTING THE FUTURE

1. *Las Vegas Review-Journal,* October 9, December 26, 1944, January 4, March 25, 1945.

2. Jamie Coughtry, ed., *Lubertha Johnson: Civil Rights Efforts in Las Vegas, 1940s–1960s;* Elizabeth Nelson Patrick, "The Black Experience in Southern Nevada."

3. Dedee Nave, "The Morelli House: Mid-century Architecture Opens to the Public," *Preservation Association of Clark County Newsletter* (ca. 2007), on file at the State Historic Preservation Office, Carson City.

4. Alan Hess, "Our Living Heritage."

5. *Las Vegas Mercury,* February 16, 2001.

6. O. Richard Norton, *The Planetarium and Atmospherium: An Indoor Universe.*

7. *Nevada State Journal,* January 13, 1963.

8. *Reno Gazette-Journal,* November 15, 1963, November 30, 1983.

9. In 2009, University of Nevada, Reno's Milton Glick refused to sign covenants within the Commission for Cultural Affairs' funding agreement, returning the awarded grant. The property is included here because the commission made the initial award.

8 ■ LEARNING FROM REMNANTS OF THE PAST

1. *Reno Gazette-Journal,* December 7, 1996.

2. This is based on the personal observations and recollections of Ronald M. James.

3. *Las Vegas Sun,* August 10, 2001; Pasquale and Crockett, "End of the Line?"

4. *Las Vegas Sun,* March 3, 1997, July 25, 26, 2000.

5. *Reno Gazette-Journal,* July 19, 1998; "Reno Is Artown," http://www.artown.org /about/about_hist.html.

6. Observations regarding the closing of the Huntridge and its sale are from the authors, who were either eyewitnesses to the events or gained insight about them from people including Richard Lenz, who was the art director at the theater during its successful years.

Bibliography

Abbe, Donald R. *Austin and the Reese River Mining District.* Reno: University of Nevada Press, 1985.

Angel, Myron. *History of Nevada, 1881.* Oakland, Calif.: Thompson and West, 1881.

Arrington, Leonard J., Feramorz Y. Fox, and Dean L. May. *Building the City of God: Community and Cooperation Among the Mormons.* Salt Lake City: Deseret Book, 1976.

Arrington, Leonard J., and Richard Jensen. "Panaca: Mormon Outpost Among the Mining Camps." *Nevada Historical Society Quarterly* (Winter 1975): 209–10, 215.

Bancroft, Hubert Howe. *The Works of Hubert Howe Bancroft.* Vol. 25, *The History of Nevada, Colorado, and Wyoming, 1540–1888.* San Francisco: History Company, 1890.

Bengali, Shashank. "Williams the Conqueror." *USC Trojan Family Magazine* (Spring 2004): 27–35.

Billington, Ray Allen. *Frederick Jackson Turner: Historian, Scholar, Teacher.* New York: Oxford University Press, 1973.

Bogue, Allan G. *Frederick Jackson Turner: Strange Roads Going Down.* Norman: University of Oklahoma Press, 1998.

Bond, Max. "Still Here: Three Architects of Afro-America—Julian Francis Abele, Hilyard Robinson, and Paul R. Williams." *Harvard Design Magazine* (Summer 1997): 1–5.

Botsford, Louise Walther. "Valentine Walther." *Northeastern Nevada Historical Society Quarterly* (1989).

Brooks, Juanita. *Dudley Leavitt: Pioneer to Southern Utah.* St. George, Utah: Self-published, 1942.

Brown, Mrs. Hugh. *Lady in Boomtown: Miners and Manners on the Nevada Frontier.* Reno: University of Nevada Press, 1991.

Bryant, Edwin. *What I Saw in California.* Introduction by Thomas D. Clark. 1848. Reprint, Lincoln: University of Nebraska Press, 1985.

Burton, Richard F. *The City of the Saints, and Across the Rocky Mountains to California.* Edited by Fawn M. Brodie. New York: Alfred A. Knopf, 1963.

Carlson, Helen S. *Place Names of Nevada: A Geographic Dictionary.* Reno: University of Nevada Press, 1974.

Cerveri, Doris. *With Curry's Compliments: The Story of Abraham Curry, Founder of Nevada's Capital City and Father of the Carson City Mint.* Elko, Nev.: Nostalgia Press, 1990.

Corbett, Pearson Starr. "Settling the Muddy River Valley." *Nevada Historical Society Quarterly* (Fall 1975).

Coughtry, Jamie, ed. *Lubertha Johnson: Civil Rights Efforts in Las Vegas, 1940s–1960s.* Reno: Oral History Program, 1988.

Edwards, Jerome E. *Patrick McCarran: Political Boss of Nevada.* Reno: University of Nevada Press, 1982.

Elliott, Russell R. *Growing Up in a Company Town: A Family in the Copper Camp of McGill, Nevada.* Reno: Nevada Historical Society, 1990.

———. *The Turn of the Century Mining Boom.* 1966. Reprint, Reno: University of Nevada Press, 1988.

Elliott, Russell R., with the assistance of William D. Rowley. *History of Nevada.* 2d ed. Lincoln: University of Nebraska Press, 1987.

Faragher, John Mack. "'A Nation Thrown Back Upon Itself': Frederick Jackson Turner and the Frontier." In *Rereading Frederick Jackson Turner*, edited by John Mack Faragher. New Haven: Yale University Press, 1994.

Fleming, Robin. "Picturesque History and the Medieval in Nineteenth-Century America." *American Historical Review* (October 1995): 1061–94.

Fowler, Don D., and David B. Madsen. "Prehistory of the Southeastern Area." In *Handbook of North American Indians.* Vol. 11, *Great Basin.* Washington, D.C.: Smithsonian Institution, 1986.

Frady, Steven R. *Jump Her Lively, Boys: An Introduction to the Fire Departments of the Comstock Lode.* Virginia City, Nev.: Liberty Engine Company No. 1, 1998.

Gomes, John M. "Golconda's Glory Days, 1898–1910." *Nevada Historical Society Quarterly* (Summer 2007): 145–67.

Gratton-Aiello, Carolyn. "New St. Joseph, Nevada: The Muddy Mission Experience Revisited." *Nevada Historical Society Quarterly* (Spring 1986).

Griffith, Martin. "What's Nevada's Oldest Town?" *Nevada Magazine* (September–October 1998): 10–15, 76–77.

Hall, Shawn. *A Guide to the Ghost Towns and Mining Camps of Nye County, Nevada.* New York: Dodd, Mead, 1981.

———. *Old Heart of Nevada: Ghost Towns and Mining Camps of Elko County.* Reno: University of Nevada Press, 1998.

Harmon, Mella Rothwell, and Guy L. Rocha. "Foreman-Roberts House." National Register of Historic Places nomination amendment, 2005.

Harvey, Elizabeth Safford. "Icon of Community: The Manhattan Schoolhouse." *Nevada Historical Society Quarterly* (Summer 2006).

Heller, Dean. *Political History of Nevada*. 11th ed. Carson City: State Printing Office, 2006.

Hess, Alan. "Our Living Heritage." *Architecture Las Vegas* (2007): 24–26.

Historic American Buildings Survey. "Kiel Ranch, North Las Vegas, Nevada." HABS, no. 19 (1988).

Hollister, Joyce. "Old School Ties." *Nevada Magazine* (September–October 2003).

Hopkins, A. D., and K. J. Evans, eds. *The First 100: Portraits of the Men and Women Who Shaped Las Vegas*. Las Vegas: Huntington Press, 1999.

Hulse, James W. *Lincoln County, Nevada, 1864–1909: History of a Mining Region*. Reno: University of Nevada Press, 1971.

———. *The Silver State: Nevada's Heritage Reinterpreted*. Reno: University of Nevada Press, 1991.

Hummel, N. A. *General History and Resources of Washoe County, Nevada*. Reno: Nevada Educational Association, 1988.

Igler, David. *Industrial Cowboys: Miller and Lux and the Transformation of the Far West, 1850–1920*. Berkeley and Los Angeles: University of California Press, 2001.

Jackson, Nicholas D. "A History of the Stewart Indian School." Master's thesis, University of Nevada–Reno, 1969.

James, Ronald M. "Defining the Group: Nineteenth-Century Cornish on the Mining Frontier." In *Cornish Studies 2*, edited by Philip Payton. Exeter, UK: University of Exeter Press, 1994.

———. "Home Away From Home: Cornish Immigrants in Nineteenth-Century Nevada." In *Cornish Studies 15*, edited by Philip Payton. Exeter, UK: University of Exeter Press, 2008.

———. *The Roar and the Silence: A History of Virginia City and the Comstock Lode*. Reno: University of Nevada Press, 1994.

———. *Temples of Justice: County Courthouses of Nevada*. Reno: University of Nevada Press, 1994.

James, Ronald M., and Susan A. James. *Castle in the Sky: George Whittell Jr. and the Thunderbird Lodge*. 2d ed. Lake Tahoe: Thunderbird Lodge Press, 2005.

James, Ronald M., and Michelle McFadden. "Remnants of the National Youth Administration in Nevada." *Nevada Historical Society Quarterly* (Fall 1991).

James, Susan A. "Shakespeare and Bear Fights." *Nevada Magazine* (May–June 2001): 20–23.

———. *Virginia City's Historic Fourth Ward School: From Pride to Glory.* Virginia City, Nev.: Fourth Ward School Museum, 2003.

Jerrems, Jerry. "Railroads West, Boulder City Depot Restoration." Report on file with the Commission for Cultural Affairs, 1999.

Koval, Anna B., and Katherine Boyne. *Peter Dalton Ranch (Joseph Ferretto Ranch).* Historic American Building Survey, No. NV-22, on file at the State Historic Preservation Office, Carson City.

Land, Barbara, and Myrick Land. *A Short History of Reno.* Reno: University of Nevada Press, 1995.

Leavitt, Francis H. "The Influence of the Mormon People in the Settlement of Clark County." Master's thesis, University of Nevada–Reno, 1934.

Leavitt, Violet. "The History of the Virgin Valley." In *Nevada State Historical Society Papers, 1923–1924.* Reno: Nevada State Historical Society, 1924.

Lewis, Oscar. *The Town That Died Laughing: The Story of Austin, Nevada, Rambunctious Early-Day Mining Camp and of Its Renowned Newspaper, the "Reese River Reveille."* 1955. Reprint, Reno: University of Nevada Press, 1986.

Lillard, Richard Gordon. *Desert Challenge: An Interpretation of Nevada.* New York: Alfred A. Knopf, 1942.

McBride, Dennis. "Grand Canyon–Boulder Dam Tours, Inc.: Southern Nevada's First Venture Into Commercial Tourism." *Nevada Historical Society Quarterly* (Summer 1984).

———. *In the Beginning: A History of Boulder City, Nevada.* 2d ed. Boulder City: Hoover Dam Museum, 1992.

McBride, Terri. *Exploration and Early Settlement in Nevada.* Carson City: Nevada Historic Preservation Office, 2002.

McCracken, Robert D. *A History of Tonopah, Nevada.* Tonopah, Nev.: Nye County Press, 1990.

McDonald, Russell. "The Development of Lovelock." *Nevada Historical Society Quarterly* (Winter 1976): 261–64.

Meeks, Carrol L. V. "Romanesque Before Richardson in the United States." *Art Bulletin* (March 1953): 17–33.

Millard, Arnold A. *History of the Carson Brewing Company: "Nevada's Oldest Business."* Carson City, Nev.: Brewery Press, 1980.

Mumford, Mark. "Form Follows Nature: The Origins of American Organic Architecture." *Journal of Architectural Education* (Spring 1989).

Myrick, David F. *Railroads of Nevada and Eastern California.* Vols. 1–2. Reno: University of Nevada Press, 1992.

Nicoletta, Julie. *Buildings of Nevada.* Oxford: Oxford University Press, 2000.

Norton, O. Richard. *The Planetarium and Atmospherium: An Indoor Universe.* Healdsburg, Calif.: Naturegraph Publishers, 1968.

Oldham, Wilda. *Carson City: Nevada's Capital City.* Genoa, Nev.: Desk Top Publishers, 1991.

Paher, Stanley W. *Las Vegas: As It Began—as It Grew.* Las Vegas: Nevada Publications, 1971.

Pasquale, Verona, and Cheryl Rose Crockett. "The End of the Line? The Railroad Cottages of Las Vegas, Then and Now." *Nevada Historical Society Quarterly* (Winter 1984).

Patrick, Elizabeth Nelson. "The Black Experience in Southern Nevada." Pts. 1 and 2. *Nevada Historical Society Quarterly* (Summer and Fall 1979).

Patterson, Edna, Louise A. Ulph, and Victor Goodwin. *Nevada's Northeast Frontier.* Sparks, Nev.: Western Printing and Publishing, 1969.

Peters, Natalie D. "The American One-Room Schoolhouse: A Study of a Community Vernacular Building Artifact." *Thresholds in Education* (2001): 39–44.

Pickering, Lee Lukes. *The Story of St. Mary's Art Center Now and St. Mary Louise Hospital Then.* Carson City, Nev.: St. Mary's Art Center, 1986.

Piper's Opera House. *Bringing Piper's Into the 21st Century.* Virginia City, Nev.: Piper's Opera House, 1999.

Reeve, W. Paul. "The Virgin River Doused Cotton Mission Settlers' Hopes." *History Blazer* (October 1995).

Reid, John B., and Ronald M. James. *Uncovering Nevada's Past: A Primary Source History of the Silver State.* Reno: University of Nevada Press, 2004.

Robrish, Dan. "A Town's Time Capsule." *Nevada Magazine* (September–October 1996): 86.

Rowley, William D. "Ranching and Farming in Nevada." In *Nevada Comprehensive Preservation Plan.* Edited by William G. White, Ronald M. James, and Richard Bernstein. 2d ed. Carson City, Nev.: State Historic Preservation Office, 1991.

———. *Reno: Hub of the Washoe County.* Woodland Hills, Calif.: Windsor Publications, 1984.

Rowse, A. L. *The Cousin Jacks: The Cornish in America.* New York: Scribner, 1969.

Steiner, Harold A. "The Old Spanish Trail, 1829–1850." *Las Vegas Review Journal* (July 4, 1987).

Todd, Cecil. *The Cornish Miner in America.* 2d ed. Spokane, Wash.: A. H. Clark, 1995.

Torrence, C. W. *History of Masonry in Nevada.* Sparks, Nev.: Grand Lodge f and a.m., 1945.

Townley, John M. *Tough Little Town on the Truckee: Reno, 1868–1900.* Reno: Great Basin Studies Center, 1983.

———. *Turn This Water Into Gold: The Story of the Newlands Project.* 2d ed., with Susan A. James. Reno: Nevada Historical Society, 1998.

Turner, Frederick Jackson. "The Problem of the West." In *The Frontier in American History*, 205–21. New York: Henry Holt, 1953.

———. "The Significance of the Frontier in American History." In *The Frontier in American History*, 1–38. New York: Henry Holt, 1953.

———. "The Significance of the Section in American History." In *Rereading Frederick Jackson Turner*, edited by John Mack Faragher. New Haven: Yale University Press, 1994.

Van Trump, James D. "The Romanesque Revival in Pittsburg." *Journal of the Society of Architectural Historians* (October 1957).

Venturi, Robert, Denise Scott Brown, and Steven Izenour. *Learning From Las Vegas.* Cambridge: mit Press, 1972.

Williams, Raymond. *Marxism and Literature.* Oxford: Oxford University Press, 1977.

Wren, Thomas. *A History of the State of Nevada: Its Resources and People.* New York: Lewis Publishing, 1904.

Wright, Frank. *Wildcat Country: Las Vegas High School and Its Neighborhood, 1930–1945.* Las Vegas: Nevada State Museum and Historical Society, 1989.

Wurm, Ted, and Harre Demoro. *The Silver Short Line: A History of the Virginia and Truckee Railroad.* Virginia City, Nev.: Virginia and Truckee Railroad, 1983.

Zanjani, Sally. *Devils Will Reign: How Nevada Began.* Reno: University of Nevada Press, 2006.

———. *Goldfield: The Last Gold Rush on the Western Frontier.* Athens: Ohio University Press, Swallow Press, 1922.

Zanjani, Sally, and Guy Louis Rocha. *The Ignoble Conspiracy: Radicalism on Trial in Nevada.* Reno: University of Nevada Press, 1986.

Index